READY TO RESTORE

THE LAYMAN'S GUIDE TO CHRISTIAN COUNSELING

Jay E. Adams

Presbyterian and Reformed Publishing Co.
Phillipsburg, New Jersey 08865

To John Bettler
A warm friend and trusted colleague:
The hidden force behind nouthetic counseling

Brothers, even if a person is caught in some trespass, you who have the Spirit should restore him in a spirit of meekness, watching out for yourself so that you won't be tempted too (Gal. 6:1).

CONTENTS

PREFACE

All Christians must counsel; I have shown this in *Competent to Counsel* and in *The Big Umbrella*. Again, in chapter 1 of this book I shall investigate that subject in a slightly different way. Since it is true that every Christian must counsel, it is important for those of us who have been involved in doing and teaching Christian counseling to provide help in a form that is both simple and non-technical, and yet, at the same time, biblical and fairly comprehensive. That is a difficult balance to achieve, I recognize, but it is precisely what is needed. This book is my attempt to meet that need.

But before proceeding further, let me say two things plainly:

1. Reading this book will not itself make you a good counselor. My hope, nevertheless, is that it will get you started in the right direction and that it will assist you in becoming much more effective. The application of biblical principles, prayerfully perfected through persistent practice, is required; the study of a book alone will not do the job. What I have in mind in writing this book is to acquaint you with a number of these principles, and to guide you in putting them into practice. But I cannot do for you what you, in prayerful, obedient practice must do before God and your neighbor by yourself.

2. Secondly, though this book is fairly comprehensive in its scope, necessarily many areas had to be omitted in order to make it simple and easy for laymen to use as a *beginning* textbook. That means that I have by-passed many details and have tried to keep from delving into any subject too deeply.[1] But unlike many simple books, this one is neither simplistic nor superficial. Everything in it is the fruit of arduous Bible study as well as a long and successful ministry of the Word in counseling. I have made every effort to produce a book that is free of all the unnecessary complications of technical jargon and tedious argumentation but that (at the same time) preserves and presents a true picture of Christian counseling in a coherent and systemic way. The book is almost entirely free of polemic.

---

1. For more depth and detail see my other books; especially *Competent to Counsel, The Christian Counselor's Manual, Lectures on Counseling,* and *More than Redemption.*

Well, then, if that is the sort of book that you are now about to study, how can you use it most profitably?

Let me suggest one or two ways in which you may do so. First, it may be used as a textbook in Bible colleges, churches, Bible study groups, prayer meetings or older youth groups. The content, scope, format and language have been designed for such use. In the less formal contexts one way to structure the class would be for the teacher to assign a chapter a week for each member to read prior to attending a seminar based on that reading. He should ask each student to write out observations and questions that the reading occasioned to be presented during the seminar. When these are presented, they may be discussed. Those questions which are not adequately answered should be referred to four persons to whom has been loaned a copy of one of my four more comprehensive books mentioned in footnote no. 1. During the following week, these four persons may look up answers in these books and report on their findings at the next seminar. This procedure will acquaint the class with the existence of other, more in-depth treatments of each subject. The seminar leader should have his own copy of the four books and ought to have read the materials in all of them that are pertinent to the discussion at the upcoming seminar. Involved in the seminar discussion ought to be a number of "what if . . .?" questions, raised by individuals, or by the class, to which the whole body addresses itself. These questions ought to be concerned with the practical outworking of the biblical principles and techniques discovered in reading as they may.be applied under various circumstances to many different counseling cases. Persons in the seminar may wish to share counseling problems that they have encountered to which the chapter under discussion applies (the leader should postpone questions about matters that will be taken up in later chapters[2]). In sharing actual experiences, the leader *must* make it clear that all cases must be "flattened out." A case is flattened out when *all identifying factors* (names, dates, places, unusual characteristics, etc.) are omitted. The leader must *zealously cut off any violations of this inflexible rule*. He should break in on any account that might even *tend* to identify someone by cheerfully reminding the group of the rule. THIS RULE MUST BE OBSERVED STRICTLY. Remember, Proverbs warns continually against gossip; James 4:11 may be read and explained along with passages from the end of Ephesians 4, when

---

2. These may be written in a Seminar Agenda book for later reference. A secretary should be appointed to write up questions and be responsible for the book.

first laying down the rule prior to the first discussion period. Some groups may prefer to use role plays instead of permitting discussion of actual cases. Others may wish to do both. For this purpose, a book containing 140 counseling role-play situations has been prepared; it is entitled, *The Christian Counselor's Casebook*. At the conclusion of each seminar the seminar secretary[3] should record conclusions reached by the group in a "Book of Conclusions." These short, one-sentence conclusions should be agreed upon by the group *as a whole*. At the close of the course, the book should be xeroxed or mimeographed and made available to each member of the seminar.

Secondly, in a more formal school situation many of the procedures mentioned above might also be followed. But, in addition, the teacher may wish to assign every member *one* of the four books previously mentioned as required out-of-class reading. A term paper, reporting on that reading, plus the application of principles learned from it to one or more of the problems raised in class may be required.

Of course, there are many variations on these themes. But, if the work done attempts to supplement the emphases and materials in the book by too heavy a dependence on outside sources it will tend to defeat the design of the book. It would be better, in cases where greater scope and depth is desired, to use *More Than Redemption* plus one or more of the other three books as classroom texts.

Naturally, this book may be used for individual study as well.

I know that there is a great need for such a volume as this one; hundreds of Christian laymen, as well as their pastors, have asked me for it. In order to satisfy this need, to build up Christ's church and to honor Him as her Lord, I offer it for whatever purposes He may see fit to use it.

Jay E. Adams
The Millhouse
Juliette, Georgia
1980

---

3. See previous footnote.

Chapter One

WHO SHOULD COUNSEL?

Is Christian counseling the work of a highly specialized group of persons? Does it belong to pastors and elders of the church alone? What of everyday man or woman-in-the-pew Christians; do they too have a ministry of counseling to which God has called them as laymen? I am asked these, and dozens of similar questions that grow out of them, almost every week of the year.

The answer is simple, yet profound: God calls *every* Christian to counsel some people, somewhere, at some time about something, but He does not call him to counsel every person, under every situation, at all times about everything. I shall try to explain this statement in the rest of this chapter. In Galatians 6:1 we read:

> Brothers, even if a person is caught in some trespass, you who have the Spirit should restore him in a spirit of meekness, watching out for yourself so that you won't be tempted too.[1]

To that verse we must add Romans 15:14:

> I myself am convinced about you, my brothers, that you yourselves are full of goodness, filled with all knowledge, and competent to counsel one another.

and Colossians 3:16:

> Let Christ's Word dwell in you richly, as you teach and counsel yourselves with all wisdom, and as you sing psalms, hymns and spiritual songs with grace in your hearts toward God.

These verses plainly place all Christians (all who "have the Spirit") squarely in the business of counseling.

---

1. All New Testament quotations are from *The New Testament in Everyday English*, published separately and as the text of *The Christian Counselor's N.T.* by Baker Book House, Grand Rapids.

The command is clear: we all must "restore" any brothers or sisters whom God providentially places in our pathway day by day. But, in the same breath, there are several important considerations that we must mention. To fail to do so will leave a distorted impression of what God requires.

First, note the word "restore." This word is important. The original Greek word (the N.T. was written in Greek) was used by fishermen and by physicians when they described the mending of fishnets and the setting of fractures. They both called their work "restoration." A torn net is of little or no value; the fish easily slip through and are lost. Likewise broken bones in an arm make it useless until they are set. But when nets are repaired and bones have been mended, we say that they have been *restored to their former use.*

After restoration, the net or the limb is once more capable of functioning as it should. That, precisely, is the goal of Christian counseling that is set forth in Galatians 6:1. By bearing the burden of counseling those in need (and it is a burden to counsel) one seeks to restore an erring brother or sister to usefulness in Christ's church to His honor and their benefit (cf. Gal. 6:2 with 6:5). The counselor does not assume his brother's responsibilities for him (that isn't what v. 2 is saying); rather, he bears the burden of his brother's need for counsel *so that* the brother himself may shoulder his responsibilities (v. 5). That is restoring: restoring another to a place of usefulness in the Lord's church.

Secondly, note that the Christian layman himself is to do this restoring. He is not told to refer the brother or sister who needs counseling to the pastor or to the elders of the church. Rather, restoration is his obligation. Presumably, what Paul is sayng is that to have the Spirit basically qualifies one Christian to assist another. The fact of the Spirit's presence makes it not only possible but proper for one to initiate and to enter into the restoration (or counseling) process. That does not mean that one who gets stuck at some point or other in the course of counseling may not seek the help of another Christian[2]; of course he may. But it does mean that he may not use referral as a means of shirking his own personal responsibilities in the matter. He must remember that God providentially placed the erring Christian in *his* pathway for him to minister to. Unlike the priest and Levite, he may not pass by on the other side. God requires all of us in such situations to become good Samaritans, pouring oil on the soul at our own expense.

2. And, of course, if the one needing counseling refuses it, the concerned party may be obligated to call on the elders for help.

If at some point referral to a pastor or to an elder becomes necessary, it is wise to refer not only the counselee, but also yourself. When you do, you will learn what you didn't know so that, in the future, you will be able to handle the same sort of problem yourself. Moreover, you may be able to offer the counselor invaluable information.

Thirdly, notice also that it is those whom God has providentially placed in your pathway that you are commanded to restore. He has *not* called you to a ministry of *searching out* potential counseling cases (there is hardly any need for that; bodies are strewn all over your Jericho road!). The layman who goes *looking* for problems among his fellow Christians sins; he becomes a "busybody" (II Thess. 3:11). His task is to do good *as the opportunity arises* (Gal. 6:10); i.e., as God places persons in his way. This important qualification means that laymen are called to an informal ministry of counseling. Counseling is but an *occasional* part of the task of being a Christian. Because they have the Spirit, they are capable of doing such informal counseling as they are called upon to do in the everyday course of their life's activities. But they are *not* called to a formal ministry of counseling as a part of their *life calling*. That task is given to specially gifted men who are ordained (appointed) to that task as teaching and ruling elders who are required to shepherd God's flock.

To these official church counselors, who are required by God to counsel as a part of their office (or work), God has given a heavier burden and a broader authority that corresponds to it. As a result, they must do what the layman is forbidden to do: they must search out problems among the members of the church in order to nip them in the bud. As shepherds they are required not only to handle the problems that they stumble over along life's road, they must also keep watch over the souls (lives) of each member:

> Obey your leaders and submit to them. They are keeping watch over you as men who will have to give an account. Obey so that they may do this with joy and not as a burden, since that wouldn't be to your advantage (Heb. 13:17).

The Greek word in that verse translated "keeping watch" means to "remain awake" and to "be alert" to problems that may arise.

Moreover, laymen may counsel at the second level of the reconciliation/discipline process (Matt. 18:16) but not at the third (Matt. 18:17-20; though they may be witnesses at that level if they have participated in unsuccessful counseling at the second level). At the third level, the officers, representing

3

the whole church, forgive or excommunicate using the keys for binding and loosing (vv. 18-20). This third level, disciplinary type of counseling belongs to the "two or three" elders who are called to administer it.

While the scope , and to some extent the type, of counseling that Christian laymen do is limited, it still encompasses a large (perhaps the largest) amount of the counseling that is done in the church. Much of the third level counseling in which elders are now engaged would not have to be done if faithful, instructed laymen had known of their responsibility to counsel and had assumed it. Many of the "one another" passages in the N.T. pertain in some way to lay counseling.[3]

Because laymen who take the biblical commands to counsel seriously have such a far-reaching and important responsibility, they should study how to do so most effectively. After all, good counsel can help another immensely; poor counsel can be detrimental. The lives of brothers and sisters are at stake, as well as the welfare of Christ's church and the honor of His Name. Therefore, the command to restore must not be taken lightly.

To help you counsel better, in a more biblical way, in the next chapter we shall note some of the proper goals and attitudes that God says must accompany Christian counseling.

---

3. A good assignment for classes would be to locate, study and report on these passages.

4

Chapter Two

GOALS, ATTITUDES AND DANGERS

Counseling is neither easy nor simple. But the problems connected with it can be reduced to a minimum by carefully adhering to biblical directives. Those who fail to do so harm themselves and reduce the possibility of helping others.

Because it involves the welfare of others, how counseling is done is vital. Some, becoming aware of the dangers, withdraw altogether and disobey the command to "restore" others. God will not allow that; He has called you to this ministry as a believer. Since you may not back out of the responsibility to counsel, you must learn how to set proper goals and objectives, how to develop appropriate attitudes and how to avoid the many pitfalls inherent in the counseling situation. In a way, the entire book tries to help you do just these things, but in this chapter I shall mention one or two basic factors that will get you on the right track from the beginning.

The *ultimate* goal behind all Christian activity, including counseling, is to glorify God (Col. 3:23). Christians are never humanistic; all they do, for them, involves the vertical dimension. Nevertheless, in each endeavor, there is an overall objective that one seeks to reach *in order* to glorify God. Let us ask, then, "What is the overall objective of lay counseling?" We have already noted in the previous chapter that Paul calls us to *restore* erring brothers and sisters to their place of usefulness to Christ in His church (Gal. 6:1). Restoration to usefulness, therefore, is the objective of Christian counseling. Whenever you counsel another you must ask, "How has his usefulness to Christ been diminished by his problem?" And you must not rest until usefulness is attained.[1]

The goal of restoration ought to guide the whole of one's attitudes and activities. The counselor counsels not to punish, or to expose another's failures, or to gloat over him, etc.; he counsels to restore him to usefulness. Moreover, with this goal constantly in mind, the counselor will do what he is

---

1. Paul's work with Onesimus led him to write: "Onesimus . . . was useless to you but now has become useful both to me and to you" (vv. 10, 11). Sometimes counselors ask, "How do we know when to discontinue counseling?" One very important factor in that decision is the determination that a counselee has been restored to usefulness.

doing not only to help the counselee (as important as that may be), but also to accomplish other goals. It is perfectly correct to *care* for the counselee and to seek his welfare; apart from such caring in which the counselor may even "weep with those who weep and rejoice with those who rejoice," neither the ultimate goal (God's glory) nor the overall objective (restoration) is possible. However, Christian counselors, unlike other counselors, are not merely oriented toward the counselee; they want to honor Christ and, like Him, they also care about His body, the church. The welfare of the whole body is adversely affected by the failure of any part. Counseling, therefore, is not only an interaction between a counselor and one or more persons in a counseling room; it also interacts in any number of ways with the whole flock and all of its activities. Every counselor must see clearly that whatever he does in counseling he does not only for the counselee but also for Christ and for His church.

Counseling is an activity in which the layman engages not as a private individual, but as a member of the body. As a "one anothering" activity (cf. Col. 3:16) it is carried on among those who have mutual obligations as members of the church. Lay counseling, *as well as* counseling done by elders in an official way, is a church activity, not a personal one.[2] Lay counseling, then, while not official (i.e., not conducted in the name of the church by its officers) nevertheless is subject to the leadership of the church.

Lay counselors must be willing to receive instruction in counseling from the church, just as they would be willing to receive instruction in evangelism or in family living. On the other hand, since God requires laymen to counsel, it is incumbent upon churches to provide such instruction. If your church does not provide instruction, you should ask for it (in a kindly and helpful way). This book has been designed as a tool for churches as well as for members. Every lay counselor also must be willing to subject his counseling activities to the oversight and order of the church. No one should take it on himself to hang out a shingle and do counseling apart from the church. All lay counseling must be done as a part of one's church activities and under its authority.

To encourage lay persons to counsel as a part of their congregational life, churches might even set aside rooms in the church building that may be used by laymen who need a quiet, secluded place where counseling may be done.

---

2. Unless it is counseling among the members of one's own family. Even that has strong repercussions on church life.

6

Churches must not only discourage improper forms and modes of lay counseling, but must make every effort to encourage and structure for proper practices.

The one essential attitude, beyond the care for the counselee (mentioned already) and the concern for Christ's honor in His church, is also mentioned in Galatians 6:1; it is "the spirit [or attitude] of meekness."

Better than giving some sort of dictionary definition of meekness is an attempt to describe it for you. A proud, self-asserting, arrogant person who is prone to force his will on another is the opposite of a meek person. The latter, in contrast, is humble and gentle, but not weak. There is a greater power in his bearing than if he exerted some external force; the force is in his character and personality. He has inner strength and does not need external power. In practice, he is the opposite of the person who would say to the counselee, "Well, I see that you've been at it again," or "Well, I told you so." Rather, you are more likely to hear him say something like this: "I'm here to help you because you need it and because Christ sent me, not because I think that I am any better than you are." Indeed, his attitude is expressed most fully when he says, "I'm helping you today, but who knows whether I may need your help next week?"

This spirit or attitude of meekness comes from keeping in mind one's own inabilities and sinfulness, and from remembering that any wisdom, knowledge, skill or righteousness that he has is the result of God's grace. Such an attitude is, as Paul makes clear, the Spirit's fruit as He impresses these truths of His Word upon us (Gal. 5).

When one goes to a brother or sister in the spirit of meekness to offer counsel, he can do no harm. Even if he is rejected, and the rejection is violent, meekness will win out. The response will be unwarranted and cannot help but add to the counselee's conviction of sin. Moreover, true meekness will not allow for a hostile cross-response by the counselor. It will lead, instead, to a "soft answer" calculated to "turn away wrath" (Prov. 15:1). Lack of meekness, on the other hand, can be the occasion for further unnecessary unpleasantness that will only complicate the original problem.

But that isn't all; there is more to consider. Meekness, together with proper goals and understanding of them, will go a long way toward averting any dangers to the counselee. Of course, the counsel that he is given must be biblical, and it should be given skillfully. But since the rest of the book pertains to these matters, I should like to focus my attention solely on the matter of Paul's warning to the counselor. The key here is awareness of the possibility of falling prey to the very temptation to which the counselee himself has succumbed and the need for caution and, in some cases, to take precautionary measures.

In Galatians 6, Paul wisely points to a phenomenon in counseling that is well known to us in other areas of life. A drowning man may also drown his rescuer along with himself unless the one doing the life saving knows about this possibility and observes the proper precautions to avert it. Many counselors, for instance, have themselves become involved sexually with those whose sexual problems were the object of counseling. This phenomenon explains Jude's concern about showing mercy to others "with caution, hating even the clothing spotted from the flesh" (v. 23). One must despise and avoid the sin that has debilitated a counselee as he would the pus running from an open wound caused by an infectious disease. In all he does in counseling, he must take the utmost care to maintain righteous conditions so that he himself will not become a victim of the sinful disease. A wise counselor, therefore, will do whatever is biblically legitimate to preclude self-infection. If, in the example given above, there is the slightest possibility that a counselee might be seeking sexual involvement, even in fantasy, the counselor ought to bring in a third party to preclude any such eventuality.

In general, then, let me encourage every layman to be careful. Before entering into a counseling relationship it will be well for him to consult the following check list:
1. Do I sense that I have any spirit of antagonism, hostility or superiority toward the counselee? If so—straighten out your heart before God in repentance before proceeding.
2. What are my goals and motives in entering into counseling? Do I have a full-orbed view of what I am about to do, including a desire to please and honor God and a concern for the welfare of Christ's church as well as the wish to help the counselee? Perhaps this reminder itself, prayerfully considered, will serve to sharpen your perspective.
3. Have I considered the personal dangers in this counseling situation and adequately insulated myself from them? Are there any other precautionary measures I should take before proceeding? If necessary, postpone counseling until you have done so.

Chapter Three

WHAT IS COUNSELING?

So far, I have referred to counseling as that process by which one Christian restores another to a place of usefulness to Christ in His church. I have said that Christian counseling is an activity in which one engages primarily as a member of the church, and which, therefore, is subject to the authority and order of the elders of the church. Those statements are accurate, so far as they go, but they do not tell the whole story.

There is a N.T. Greek word for counseling (not the only one) that goes further and tells us a lot more about counseling. It is a comprehensive term that takes in most of what is said elsewhere under additional terms. That is one reason why it is important for you to thoroughly understand it. Since there is no English equivalent for this word, I shall teach you the Greek word itself together with its full meaning.

The word is *nouthesia* (pronounced "noothuhseéuh"). This is the word from which the name nouthetic (pronounced "noothéhtik") counseling comes. Nouthetic counseling, then, is simply another designation for biblical counseling.

What does the word *nouthesia* mean? It contains three elements: *change* through *confrontation* out of *concern*. It presupposes,

firstly, that there are sinful patterns and activities in the life of the counselee that God wants changed;

secondly, that this change will be brought about through a verbal confrontation of the counselee with the Scriptures as the counselor ministers them in the power of the Holy Spirit, and

thirdly, that this confrontation is done in a loving, caring, familial manner for the benefit of the counselee.

You can readily see how rich the biblical concept of *nouthesia* is. Let us now consider each of these elements separately in greater depth.

I. *Change*

All counseling aims at change. Without this element, one may be attempting to do something, but whatever that is, it isn't counseling. In the word *restore*, a term that we have studied already, that need for change is clearly implied: something (or someone) that has lost its usefulness is changed (or restored) into something (or someone) that is now, as a result, useful for the purpose for which it was made. But in counseling what is it that must be changed? And what occasions the change?

In Galatians 6:1, Paul speaks of the Christian who is "caught in sin." This situation occasions the need for change. The change that is contemplated in the restoration to usefulness is a change in his life patterns in which sinful beliefs, attitudes and behaviors are replaced by righteous ones.

All counseling has to do with changes in beliefs, judgments, values, relationships, behavior and other such moral elements of life. Sin in human life has led to distortions of life in each of these categories. It is, as a result, sinful thought and action that is the object of change in Christian counseling.

Now, when I say that we are concerned to exchange sinful patterns of thought and activity for righteous ones, I must not be misunderstood. I am not saying that all of our troubles are due to our own personal sin.[1] The cases of Job and the blind man of John 9 very clearly demonstrate the truth that many troubles in a sinful world come from sources outside of ourselves; we definitely do *not* always bring on ourselves the trouble and misery we experience. But, as in Job's case, counseling may also be needed in order to teach one how to respond to such trouble. That sort of counseling is *preventive* counseling. *Nouthesia* is *remedial* counseling.[2] *Nouthesia* refers to situations in which one has brought trouble on himself by his sin, or in which he has responded sinfully to pressures or trouble that he did not generate. It is about *nouthesia* that Paul wrote in Galatians 6:1, although, in that place, he did not use the word (a few of the places where he does use the term are: Rom. 15:14; Col. 1:28; 3:16; Acts 20:31). Lay counseling must be both preventive and remedial. But, in this book, we shall be concerned almost exclusively with nouthetic, or remedial, counseling. The person who needs *nouthesia*, in one way or another, has been thinking and acting sinfully. Nouthetic counseling aims at changing both by . . .

II. *Confrontation*

The word confrontation implies that personal, verbal (usually oral, face-

---

1. Ultimately, of course, all trouble in the world goes back to Adam's sin.

2. Unfortunately, Job's counselors attempted remedial counseling and therefore failed to help him meet this need for preventive counseling.

to-face) contact is the means used to effect the change. Moreover, this is a confrontation of a counselee by a counselor with the biblical principles that apply to his situation. There is no idea of nastiness or of harshness involved in the concept of *confrontation*. Rather, nouthetic counseling is in every way like a helpful conference in which the counselor is in charge and the subject of the conference (or consultation) is the need for change in the life of the counselee. As a matter of fact, the word is a warm term, used of parents confronting children and of brothers confronting brothers out of . . .

III. *Concern*

This element always must be present. Otherwise the confrontation will be sterile, harsh, lifeless, cold and professional. Care for another, strong desire and untiring effort to relieve him of the misery that sinful life patterns have brought upon him, are all hallmarks of biblical, nouthetic counseling.

Counseling like this seeks to effect change by the ministry of the Word. In ministering the Scriptures, one interprets and applies the precepts and practices of the Scriptures to another in an attempt to help him bring about the changes that will relieve him of his miseries. This ministry is carried on prayerfully; it is the Holy Spirit who uses His Word to illumine the mind of the one receiving it so that he becomes convicted of his sin and is directed toward the change God requires. He also asks for wisdom to minister it well and for strength for the counselee to obey it.

The goal of all Christian counseling is scriptural change leading to restoration to use. Involved in this is a change toward love. The whole Bible was written, Jesus said, to enable one to love God and to love his neighbor. All counseling pertains to establishing, reestablishing or strengthening those love relationships in one way or another.

The Bible is the book that God provided to guide us in counseling and in it is all that is needed to bring about every change required to live a life pleasing to God. It contains all things necessary for life and godliness. Listen to what Paul says in II Timothy 3:16, 17:

> All Scripture is breathed out by God and useful for teaching, for conviction, for correction and for disciplined training in righteousness, in order to make the man of God adequate, and fully to equip him for every good task.

According to those two verses it is the Bible that not only makes one wise for salvation (justification) but also becomes the source of all change in the believer (sanctification) as well. The Bible was produced by the Holy Spirit in order to bring about the very sort of change that we seek in counseling. When properly used, it will do four things:

1. TEACH

   The Bible sets the standard for faith and life (what we must believe and do). It teaches by both precept (e.g., the Ten Commandments) and example (e.g., the life of Christ) how a human being must live in order to please God.

2. CONVICT

   But as we compare our lives with the biblical standard, we come to recognize how far short of love for God and neighbor that we have come, and are convicted of our sin. All genuine change in sinful living takes place at a level of depth through conviction. Where there is no conviction, there is no biblically acceptable change.

3. CORRECT

   Confession (admission) of sin and the seeking of fatherly forgiveness from God is the next step in biblical change. This repentance, or change of mind, leads to a change of behavior.

4. TRAIN

   It is not enough to know what God requires, how far short we have fallen of those requirements and how to get out of the sin and misery into which we have plunged; we must also know how to avoid those sins and how to stay out of them in the future. That takes "disciplined training in righteousness." The counselee must be rehabituated according to the alternative patterns found in the Bible; this comes by "disciplining toward godliness" (I Tim. 4:7). We must put off the old ways and put on new ones. In no other way can one make progress in Christian living and learn how to avoid the same sins in the future.

These four steps, which the Holy Spirit brings about only through the Bible, are sufficient. Indeed, they comprise the most complete plan for change that exists. The Bible has *all* that is needed to lead to the proper changes. Paul assures us that the Bible alone can make the counselor "adequate" (v. 17). He never lacks anything if he depends on the Bible. To say it again, another way, he insists that the Bible itself will "equip him fully" for the task of changing lives. And, to make sure that no one would think that there ever might be a case in which this did not hold true, he added "for *every* good work."

In order to counsel effectively, the lay counselor must spend much time studying the Scriptures carefully so that he may minister the Word with accuracy and assurance. The proper study of counseling, as of man himself, is the Bible.

Chapter Four

READY TO RESTORE

We have been discussing the biblical requirement that every Christian must counsel. But that requirement raises other questions, one of which is, "Given the personal inadequacies in both knowledge and life of so many Christians, how could such persons counsel when they probably need counseling themselves?" It is true that in most churches discipline of both doctrine and life is either very lax or non-existent.[1] As a result, while numbers and finances are increased, life among God's people often has deteriorated. There are, naturally, notable exceptions. But where these problems exist, what does one do?

First, you must recognize that the early N.T. church was not perfect either. Sometimes we idealize the apostolic period. There were plenty of problems in the Galatian church. A study of I and II Corinthians should dispel all idealism. But, the apostles did call for discipline, and persecution soon helped to thin out of the ranks many who did not mean business. Today, neither of those purifying forces is at work among most American churches. So, what can be done?

For starters, you must realize that it isn't only perfect persons who are qualified to counsel; if that were the case, there would be no one to do the job. Obviously, at various times, one may be a counselee who, at other times, may be a counselor. The categories must not be fixed. And, remember that the *goal* is to restore every Christian counselee to usefulness, a significant part of which is an ability to counsel others. But, once more, how do we know when he is able to counsel another; or, at least, *ought* to be able to do so were he prepared?

Some think that, in order to help another, a Christian must live in the 99th percentile. Clearly, that would severely limit the number of potential counselors in the Christian community. There is no biblical warrant for drawing

---

1. This is one of the principal causes of difficulty in human lives. Were we to discipline properly, the number of counseling problems in our churches would be reduced significantly and would be caught earlier, before they became so severe.

lines on any such basis. What, then, is the principle by which we may divide those who ought to counsel from others? It is the very principle by which we ought to determine who *needs* counseling. Again, Galatians 6:1, on which we have drawn so freely already, provides the answer: *all* those who have the Spirit (i.e., all regenerate persons), who at that moment do not need to be restored themselves, ought to be ready to counsel another whom God providentially places in their pathway. If they are not ready or able, or willing to do so, they may need encouragement, instruction, rebuke, counsel or any combination of the above. That is to say, if one is not a potential counselee, he is a potential counselor. If he currently maintains usefulness to Christ in His church, fundamentally, he is in a position to help others.

But what if you are not now receiving counsel, but probably ought to be; what should you do? Ask for it. I suggest that you make an appointment with your pastor immediately or go to a Christian brother or sister whose judgment you trust. Explain your situation; ask how you can be restored to usefulness. There are very few persons who would not be overjoyed to receive your request. Every true shepherd of Christ will be willing and anxious to help you fulfil that desire.

It is possible that the Christian worker or the pastor will not be able to help you. What do you do then? Ask him to refer you to the pastor, or another pastor. And it would be good for him to accompany you when you go, so that he will learn how to handle such problems in the future. You, too, should note what is done for future reference (when you are restored, you will have to think about doing counseling too).

This book may have fallen into the hands of a Christian who is the member of a liberal church whose pastor does not believe in the Bible. You could not expect to receive biblical counseling from him. Find, instead, a conservative, Bible-believing counselor who can capably direct you from the Scriptures. And, incidentally, talk to him somewhere along the line about changing your church membership too.

Sadly, it is not only liberal pastors who give non-scriptural counsel these days. Some men, who preach the Bible in their pulpits, change their tune when they enter the counseling room. They may have been taught in seminary to counsel psychologically (i.e., according to worldly wisdom and ways) rather than scripturally. They may mix the two. Be alert; not all Christian counselors do Christian counseling. There are many Christians who are counselors; their personal faith is genuinely Christian but the counseling that they do is not. If you find yourself in a counseling session of that sort, thank the counselor for his concern, but then in a kindly way, ask for *Christian* counseling *from the Bible*. Ask: "What does *God* want me to do?" If the counselor persists in substituting worldly wisdom for biblical truth, in mixing the two, or does not know how to counsel biblically, ask him to recommend a pastor who will give you biblical counsel instead, if you don't already know whom to consult. Again, if he is willing, suggest that he accompany you.[2] In all this, be careful to maintain a loving, gentle spirit.

But let us suppose that, although you are by no means perfect, at the present time you do not think that you need counseling, at least of any extensive sort (you could use some improvement, instruction, encouragement, etc.); by our definition, that means you ought to be ready to restore others. Yet you still may feel very uncomfortable about doing so. How can you overcome these feelings of fear, apprehension, and dis-ease?

Let me suggest that you have already begun to do so. By procuring and beginning to read this book, you have taken the first steps toward relieving your apprehensions. Moreover, it is not only newness and inexperience that causes problems, but a lack of knowledge and, especially, a lack of know-how, adds to the apprehension. The study that you are now doing should help a great deal in dispelling your fears.

But it is most important to recognize that Christians do not counsel alone; that knowledge is indispensable. A Christian does not need to rely upon his own resources. He may depend upon the promised help of the Holy Spirit, the "other counselor, just like Christ," who was sent to *stand by* us. He not only counsels us, but also helps us to counsel others:

> And I will ask the Father, and He will give you another Counselor so that He may be with you forever—He is the Spirit of truth Whom the world can't receive because it doesn't see or know Him. You know Him, because He stays with you and will be in you (John 14:16, 17).

That is why Paul indicates in Galatians 6:1 that all true Christians (those "who have the Spirit") fundamentally possess the potential for doing Christian counseling. The Holy Spirit is the "Spirit of counsel" (Isa. 11:2) because it is from Him that all wisdom and all ability to do scriptural counseling flows. In other words, if you are a genuine Christian, one in whom the Holy Spirit of counsel dwells, you already have every basic

---

2. A list of persons trained in biblical counseling is maintained by The Christian Counseling and Educational Foundation, 1790 E. Willow Grove Ave., Laverock, PA., 19118; phone: (215) 884-7676.

resource for doing Christian counseling.

I say "basic resources" because I don't want you to gain any *false* impressions from the words above. There is nothing *automatic* about how ability to counsel is attained; it is not merely the *presence* of the Holy Spirit that makes one a counselor. His presence in the counselor is absolutely essential to all God-pleasing counseling, and it is that presence alone which makes biblical counseling possible. But the possibility or basic potential for Christian counseling is not the same thing as the actuality and realization of it. To be an effective counselor ready and able to restore others, there must be a prayerful willingness and obedience, coupled with diligent study of the Scriptures and a love for Christ and His church through which the Spirit works. The Holy Spirit will not zap you at 3 a.m. on Thursday so that you will wake up in the morning with a brand new ability to counsel. He makes us to be experienced counselors as we learn from His Word and obediently follow it out of love for God and our neighbors. Usually, that obedience must begin long before apprehension and fear dissipates; you must begin counseling because God says so, not because you (at last) feel like it. You often must counsel in spite of how you feel, in spite of fears and apprehension. According to James 1:25, you must not wait till your feelings shape up (if you do, you may never begin, and adverse feelings will probably grow, not lessen), but when you obey you will be blessed "in the doing" (cf. Luke 17:14).

In the final analysis, when all the rest has been scraped away, all that keeps a Christian from becoming an effective restorer of his brothers is lack of love. Love alone is strong enough to cast out fear (I John 4:18). Fear, apart from love, can become a powerful inhibition to doing God's will. Melted by the warmth of God's love, it can do no harm. When you say, "I will please God, whether I am embarrassed by doing so or not," that is love at work, overcoming fear.

"But," you ask, "I can get past the problem of consequences to me, but what of the consequences to the brother or sister I counsel; suppose I do more harm than good?" If you are always careful to advise only those things that you are absolutely certain are scriptural, if you will pray earnestly about your effort, asking God to make it His effort as well, if you are ready to admit your lack of knowledge when you don't have the answers and if all this is done in a spirit (or attitude) of meekness, you can do the other person no harm; you cannot go wrong. But those are crucial *ifs;* reread them carefully and think long and hard about the implications of each one.

17

Never guess. Never bluff. Tell the truth, even when it hurts. Admit it when you are stumped. Ask your counselee to pray that God will help you find the answer during the next week. Search hard, prayerfully, for it. If you can't discover the answer, call a more experienced Christian, or your pastor, for help. When you proceed this way, God will bless your efforts, making them His and you will be surprised at how quickly you will grow and how much you will learn. But none of this will happen unless you begin. You don't begin because you think that at last you know enough, or because you feel right about it; you begin now, because God tells you to!

Remember, your task in biblical counseling is to minister God's Word; nothing else. But when you do you are not alone; God works through it. You are never really on your own. All vital change that occurs in the one who is restored by your ministry really happens because the Spirit molds the counselee by His Word. Your counseling function is to analyze the problem in the light of God's Word, to map out a solution from the Word and to improvise ways and means for doing so that, at every point, grow out of (and are appropriate to) the Scriptures. All you do, from start to finish, is to follow God's Word, the Bible. The Spirit who inspired it, works through His Word.

"That helps," you say, "but are there qualities, in particular, that I may develop that would help prepare me for my part?" Certainly there are. We have already spoken of the essential quality of a spirit of meekness, so I shall not repeat that. Let me list three more that occur in close connection with counseling in the Bible:

1. Goodness (Rom. 15:14)
2. Knowledge of the Word (Rom. 15:14; Col. 3:16)
3. Wisdom (Col. 3:16).

Goodness, mentioned in Romans 15:14, means not so much the quality of life that you live (though certainly that is presupposed) but rather a good-hearted attitude of concern for others. It is a desire to aid and assist others in need; a good will toward others that propels you out of self-interest and toward them. Perhaps it is best demonstrated in those who heed Paul's words in Philippians 2:3, 4:

> Do nothing out of selfishness or vanity, but rather in humility consider others better than yourselves. Each of you should not only look out for his own affairs but also for the affairs of others.

This quality must be cultivated; it does not come naturally. One must begin to do so by actually *putting* others first, caring for their interests before your own, etc., as Paul indicates. Goodness doesn't suddenly appear all on its own.

Knowledge (Rom. 15:14) is knowledge of the "Word of Christ" (Col. 3:16). It comes by studying the Word. Since counseling is a ministry of the Word, and since the Holy Spirit changes people by means of the Word, an ever-increasing knowledge of the Word is essential. The effective counselor is one who has a rich personal possession of biblical knowledge. Yet one must not wait until he thinks that he knows everything before he begins counseling. *He studies and counsels at the same time.* Each helps the other. Counseling often gives incentive and direction to study, just as the latter provides data and information for use in counseling.

And, one must study with a view to using what he learns in his own life first. That is one important way to learn how to counsel others (cf. II Cor. 1:6, 7). There is much in this book about counseling; as you study it begin to use it first in your own life. Nothing I know of will make you more ready to restore others. All of which leads to the third quality.

Wisdom. Wisdom comes from the "Word of Christ" dwelling in you richly (Col. 3:16). Wisdom is *knowledge in life.* It is not enough for you or your counselee merely to *know what God says;* you must learn how to incarnate truth and belief into day-by-day living. The more proficient one becomes in using and (especially) implementing biblical truth in day-by-day living, the more apt he will be to help others to do so too. So, your task is to become what you ought to be; that is the most essential factor in the life of one who wants to be ready to restore others.

Chapter Five

WHAT ABOUT UNBELIEVERS?

"So far you have talked only about counseling believers. You've referred to counseling as sanctification, spoken of it as a process in which Christians put off sinful patterns and put on righteous ones, etc. But what about unbelievers? How do you counsel them—or *do* you?"

No you must not try to counsel unbelievers because you cannot. If our desire in counseling is to effect change that is pleasing to God, then it is utterly impossible to counsel unbelievers.

Unbelievers have no desire to serve Christ as Lord (I Cor. 12:3b), they have no ability to understand the Scriptures (I Cor. 2), and no power to do God's will (Rom. 5:6). Instead, they have a heart of stone that is untouchable and unmoldable until the Spirit turns it into a heart of flesh (Ezek. 11:19). Unless God's regenerating Spirit is poured into that heart, transforming it, the unbeliever cannot love God or neighbor (Rom. 5:5) or follow any of God's commands (Ezek. 11:20). Clearly, then, since problems flow from the sinful heart (Matt. 15:19, 20) the unconverted heart stands in the way of all true counseling as a formidable factor that cannot be ignored.

In the Bible, the heart doesn't stand for the emotions or feelings as it does today in our culture. On the contrary, in the Bible's frame of reference one thinks with the heart, speaks to himself in his heart, lays plans in the heart, reasons, schemes, etc. Indeed, the Bible *identifies* the heart with the intellectual processes rather than sets these apart from and over against the heart as we sometimes do in our phrase ". . . we need more heart knowledge and less head knowledge." In Scripture, the head and heart are *never* set over against each other that way. The viscera are identified with the emotions in the Bible, and it is the lips, the mouth, the hands, and the outer appearance that are contrasted with the heart. The biblical concept of the heart, therefore, is the idea of the inner life that one lives before God and himself.

It is from the heart that all counseling problems spring. Consequently, it does no good whatever to attempt to change an unbeliever unless you first change his heart. To effect change otherwise is to produce outer change only.

Any counseling attempted with an unbeliever, therefore, ends in serving several bad ends, among which are:

1. Mere outer conformity to the Bible (hypocrisy). We may never encourage hypocrisy.
2. Misleading the unbelieving counselee into thinking that what he has done has pleased God when, in fact, it has not.
3. Giving the unbeliever false assurance.
4. Setting up the non-Christian for another fall; outer change will not really solve his problem.
5. Misrepresenting what God has to offer by substituting human reformation for spiritual transformation.

What, then, can be done for an unbeliever? He cannot be counseled in any Christian sense of the word because biblical counseling involves change in the heart leading to change in the life by which the Holy Spirit makes a regenerate person in some way more like Christ. What can be done then? The unbeliever may be *precounseled*. "Precounseled? What is that?"

Precounseling is a word that we use with the unbeliever. Among ourselves, precounseling is known as evangelism.

Precounseling is the task of presenting Christ to believers as the doorway not only to eternal life, but also as the way to reach solutions to their problems in this life.

So, in precounseling unbelievers, the Christian counselor must make it abundantly clear from the outset that he has not yet begun to counsel, and that, under the circumstances, it is not possible to do so. Any and all confusion about this matter must be cleared up for the unbeliever. He must be told as early as it is appropriate to do so that precounseling must precede counseling and that counseling will follow only if precounseling is successful. A use of the word precounseling will help him to distinguish it from counseling in the unbeliever's mind. As this is discussed, he must be told of his sin and his need for a Savior. The gospel must be presented. During this discussion, at some point, it might be helpful to say something like this:

"So you see, God has answers to all your problems, and I shall be happy to talk to you about them as soon as it is possible to do so. But those answers are all on the other side of a wall that separates you from them. You may not avail yourself of them until first you pass through the door in that wall. That door, of course, is the One about whom I have been speaking to you: Jesus Christ."

But when you say such things in a counseling/precounseling context, it must be done in such a way that the unbeliever is brought to genuine repentance and faith in Christ; special care must be taken to guard against obtaining mere verbal assent as a gimmick to obtain some personal end.

When after adequate precounseling, an unbeliever refuses to trust Christ as Savior, what can be done? I always weave a brief, pointed Scripture portion into the final counseling session as often as I can (15-25 times whenever possible). The passage I use is Proverbs 13:15b: "the way of the transgressor is hard." I say such things as, "So, when you leave here without Christ you will begin to discover that the way of the transgressor is hard . . . And when you begin to find out that the way of the transgressor is hard, then. . . ."

My purpose in doing this is by repetition to stick that verse like a burr under his saddle to continue to work on him as he rides off into the sunset. I have had some persons return later on who said, "I found out that the way of the transgressor is hard."

So, remember, don't even try to counsel an unbeliever. If you attempt to do so, you will only mislead him and misrepresent God.

But Who Is an Unbeliever?

Because of lack of church discipline, today this question is rarely answered satisfactorily. Therefore, let me give you some guidelines for making a decision in counseling contexts.

In general, we may say that an unbeliever is a person who has never been regenerated by the Holy Spirit and who, therefore, has never put his faith in the Lord Jesus Christ for salvation. An unbeliever is one who does not believe the gospel.

But that doesn't help us very much when it comes to actually deciding among cases, so let us try to articulate some principles for making that determination. We shall begin with three:

1. We are never allowed to make a *final judgment* about the actual state of another who professes faith in Christ. "Man looks on the outward appearance"; only God has the ability to "look on the heart" and make such final judgments.
2. All our judgments about such persons, therefore, must be *functional judgments*. That is, we make a judgment about how *we* must relate to

these persons and how we must function in that relationship. As we have seen, this functional judgment is important for deciding whether to counsel or to precounsel. This idea of a *functional* judgment emerges plainly in Matthew 18:17: "treat him *as* a heathen" (i.e., exactly as you would an unbeliever). We do not pronounce him to *be* a heathen—we cannot know his heart. He may be a very disobedient Christian. But because at the moment he gives no evidence of a willingness to submit to the authority of Christ in the Scriptures, we must relate to him *as* we would to a heathen.

3. If a person, who does not profess faith in Christ, is a member of a false religion or declares himself an atheist or an agnostic, then on the basis of his own word and his professed allegiances, we may agree with him that he is not a Christian.

So far, so good. But what about those who are members of a Bible-believing church, but whose lives show little evidence of salvation? We have no right to deal with them as unbelievers until they, or the church, declare that we may. There should be no personal judgments in this case. Here are guidelines for handling the problem:

1. After church discipline has failed (Matt. 18:15-17), in which the person has demonstrated a rejection of Christ's authority at all levels, you must make the functional judgment "I shall treat him in counseling 'as a heathen.' " You must do so, no matter what he protests.

2. If a person *claims* to be a Christian but refuses to submit to the care and discipline of Christ's church by remaining outside of the visible church, he must, nevertheless, be treated by a counselor "as a heathen."

3. If a person renounces the authority of Christ by leaving the church (I John 2:19) he may be treated "as a heathen."

The one thread running throughout all is the principle of submission to Christ's authority in the Scriptures; all turns on that.

Chapter Six

THE COUNSELING PROCESS

I have already said a few things about two aspects of the counseling process. I have discussed the four biblical steps for change and have alluded to the put on/put off dynamic for altering habit patterns. But beyond that, little else has been said.

Let us consider, in the course of a typical 8-10 week marriage counseling case, some (not all) of the sorts of things that might happen and what the interrelationships of these activities might be.

To begin with, both parties would be invited to come to counseling *together*. There is no sense whatever in scheduling separate appointments for each. Not only do separate appointments lead to more partial and untrue data, because the other party isn't present to correct and amplify what his partner says (in accordance with Prov. 18:17), but bringing them in individually occasions unnecessary suspicion and creates a situation that tends toward the temptation for one to talk negatively about another behind his back (something that is forbidden in the Scriptures). Moreover, the actual dynamics of communication between them are more readily exposed in joint sessions, and genuine biblical communication and commitments can best be begun within the structure of the counseling hour.

Typically, both should come half an hour ahead of time the first week. It will take them from 20 to 30 minutes to fill out the Personal Data Inventory forms.[1] These forms will then be reviewed by the counselor prior to admitting the counselees into the counseling room.[2] This will take him about 5-7 minutes. With a red pen he will mark items he may wish to discuss in the following session. The preliminary review will give him some tentative ideas about the counselees and about their problems, ideas that he will want to explore further in the session to follow. The form also will raise questions that he may wish to ask then, or later on.

---

1. See copy in Appendix A. These forms are available in *The Christian Counselor's Starter Packet*, C.S.S., 1790 E. Willow Grove Ave., Laverock, PA 19118.
2. Use of the P.D.I. is fully explained in *Update on Christian Counseling*, vol. I.

When the counselees enter the room, they are greeted, seated and (perhaps) a pleasantry or two is passed. But very quickly the counselor gets down to business. He begins with the P.D.I. (unless something that the counselees say or do provides an opening that he should not miss). The counselor takes charge in the spirit of Proverbs 18:15. He knows where he is going, what he needs to know and moves straight for it.

Beginning with any data written on the P.D.I. that are not clear to him, if there be such, or with any facts mentioned there that need amplification, the counselor asks direct questions to discover what he needs to know. Here are some typical samples:

1. "I see here that you've been arrested. Can you tell me something more about that?"
2. "You say that you've been taking tranquillizers; tell me, which tranquillizer do you take, and what is its effect on you?"
3. "You note here that you have had many severe emotional upsets. How about describing a couple of these."

Having satisfied himself about such matters, the counselor may turn to the counselees' replies to the first of the three basic questions asked on the final page of the P.D.I., "What is your problem?" However, if questioning prior to this leads to important data, he may wish to postpone doing so in order to follow the previous discussion to its fullest end.

The answer to the question "What is your problem?" given by each of the counselees is important. He will want to read these out loud so that each may know what the other has written. Then, he will note any significant comparisons and contrasts or agreements between these answers. An in-depth discussion of the various viewpoints with appropriate questions aimed at exploring the situation as fully as possible usually ensues.

If the counselor has spotted anything on the P.D.I. or in the counselees' manner that would indicate a lack of hope in one or both of the counselees, he may wish to postpone data gathering and, instead, work on generating hope. In such cases, a homework assignment designed to unearth whatever data could not be obtained by questioning during the counseling session itself would probably be given.

Fundamentally, hope is generated by pointing counselees to the certain promises of God in the Scriptures. In Romans 15:13, the Bible designates God as "the God of hope," and Paul calls upon God to fill the Roman Christians with "an abundance of hope by the power of the Holy Spirit."

But that hope which comes from God, who is its source, does not come out of the sky. As Paul noted earlier, in Romans 15:4,

> Whatever was written before was written for our instruction, that by the endurance and the encouragement that the Scriptures give us we may have hope.

It is through the Scriptures, then, in one way or another, that this hope is generated in the lives of counselees.

The biblical word "hope," as is clear from its use in Titus 2:13, is not the hope-so hope of modern English. None of the uncertainty of the modern term adheres to it. To understand the words "the blessed hope" as "the blessed hope-so" is, of course, totally unacceptable. The blessed hope is a certainty toward which Christians look with confident expectation. We *know* that Christ will return as that "Great God and Savior"; there is no doubt about it because God has said so in His infallible Word. So, in modern English, the blessed hope is the "joyous anticipation" or "happy expectation." Hope, in the Bible, is directed toward a certainty; it is based on God's unfailing promises. What makes it hope, as Paul explained in Romans 8:24, 25, is simply the fact that it has not yet been realized.

The counselor is able to give hope when (1) he himself believes God's promises and (2) when he is able to communicate these promises to his counselees with assurance. Any doubts on the part of the counselor can interfere very severely with the counselee's hope. Only the Christian counselor can offer such hope since only he has the certainty of the written, inerrant words of God upon which to base his assurances. For the counselor himself to intrude any doubt is a serious failing that not only does disservice to the counselee but also gravely dishonors God.

The easiest thing to do in the first session is to gather data. And many counselors do so, even when they recognize that the counselee lacks hope. But in such a case it isn't the wise thing to do. A Salvation Army officer once handed me a razor blade at the close of our first counseling session together and said, "If you hadn't given me hope, I was going to leave here and use it on my wrists." The rule is: whenever you suspect that a counselee needs hope, drop everything else and work on hope. Without hope, there is no assurance that a counselee will endure (cf. I Thess. 1:3). You may have pages full of data in your notes, but no counselee.

When the counselee is hopeful, typically the counselor will focus on data gathering. If he tries to prescribe biblical solutions to a problem that he does not understand adequately he is a "fool" and deserves to be "reproached" (cf. Berkeley version of Prov. 18:3), just as Job's counselors were. Yet even with plenty of time and a good exchange of questions and answers usually the counselor will hold most of his early conclusions in a tentative way. He will want to test them out by reading the responses to some homework assignments that he will give which are based on these conclusions. All data should be interpreted, categorized and stated in biblical terminology.

In this first session, the counselor also will wish to discover and deal with any agenda problems. If the counselee's goals differ from biblical ones, as so often is the case, these must be negotiated as soon as possible. Otherwise, in everything they attempt the counselor and the counselee will be speaking and walking past each other in opposite directions rather than side by side.

Typical of the kind of agenda problem I refer to is the following:

Counselor: "I see on your P.D.I. in answer to the question 'What do you want us to do?' you say, 'Get my wife to return at all cost. I'll do anything to get her back.'"

Counselee: "That's right—anything!"

Counselor: "Anything? Would you lie, steal, murder?"

Counselee: "Well, . . . you know what I mean."

Counselor: "No, I don't. I'm trying to find out exactly what you would and would not do. That could be important."

Counselee: "Well, . . . I guess I'm not really sure."

Counselor: "Let me put it this way; what you should say is, 'I'll do whatever God wants me to do about this problem.' "

Counselee: "I never thought of it that way. But I guess that's right."

Counselor: "Not only must counseling proceed on that basis, but we must go even a step further. As good and as proper as your concern to be reunited to your wife is, even that must not be your top priority. Otherwise it may turn out that you will be hypocritically trying gimmicks. We don't want that."

Counselee: "What do you mean?"

Counselor: "Just this: You must be willing to do *whatever* God wants you to do in this situation simply *to please God*—because He wants you to— whether your wife returns or not. You cannot make changes merely to get her back. Repentance[3] can never be a gimmick. Only if you truly repent of any sin in your life will you be able to handle either outcome: her return or her failure to return. But either way, you will be in a position of strength before God that will enable you to face whatever ensues. Your top priority must be to please God. You can do that whether she returns or not."

Such agenda negotiation is absolutely vital to enable a person to cut a straight path toward God's goals for counseling.

The final phase of a first session typically deals with the giving of various written homework assignments that grow out of the discussions during the hour. These must be carefully stated (clear, full, precise) and fully explained (often it is wise to ask a counselee to repeat the assignment for you to make sure he/she understands it). The counselor calls for commitment to the biblical goals toward which these assignments are directed, encourages the counselee and seals the commitment in prayer. The homework assignments are written in a homework book.[4]

Of course, almost anything else could happen in a first session; counselees differ. Counselors must be flexible and meet needs as they see them. But these items that I have listed are all ingredients that make a good mix for most first counseling sessions:

1. generating hope
2. gathering data
3. negotiating agenda
4. assigning homework
5. gaining commitment

There is a sixth item that I have not yet mentioned because I want to emphasize it as separate from and yet a part of all the rest. Indeed, it is the most essential element of all. Above all else, the counselor must help the counselee to put Christ in His rightful place in the center of the problem.

Most counselees come thinking and acting like pagans even though they are Christians. That's one reason why some are there. They talk as if the problem had little or no relationship to Christ and that His part is merely to get them out of the mess. Instead, the biblical counselor, with Paul (cf. Phil. 1:13), must insist that Christ is not only in the solution but also in the problem. The problem exists, not only because of somebody's sin, but also

---

3. For more on repentance see my *More Than Redemption*, pp. 215ff.
4. Available from Christian Study Services, 1790 E. Willow Grove Ave., Laverock, PA 19118.

(providentially) because in one way or another, Christ wants to do some good thing by means of it (Rom. 8:28). When a counselee begins to recognize this and looks at all aspects of the situation from that vantage point, everything takes on a new hue. When a counselee leaves the session with the thought in mind, "God is up to something good in this problem; I wonder what?," the counselor has been effective.

In the weeks that follow it is harder to describe what might take place; counseling may follow so many different courses. But there are some big themes and patterns that usually develop. I shall note a few.

At the beginning of each session, the counselor asks about the homework given at the previous session. Sometimes half a session may be devoted to this matter; occasionally, an entire session. Always, it is given careful attention. The counselor checks up on how well it was carried out, discusses failures, the reasons for these failures, reassigns homework not properly done (sometimes redesigned or restated), gives further help for completing it successfully, gathers data, gives new assignments based on past perform- ance and present commitments, acknowledges and encourages progress and deals firmly with lack of it. In all of this, he stresses the importance of discipline and the necessity for following up on one's commitments to God.

A close examination of the last paragraph will disclose the fact that in biblical counseling a strong emphasis is placed on the period *between* counseling sessions. The session itself isn't viewed as the magic hour when the expert does it for the counselee (or to him). Rather, it is the week before and after the session that is in view; the discussion is about how the counselee did before God and his neighbor and about what he must do during the week to come.

In many other kinds of counseling counselees become dependent on the counselor, and the high points are the one hour, one-day-per-week sessions with him; the week between is a sagging low point. Counseling looks like this:

Sessions   1   2   3   4   5   ♦etc.

Weeks
Between
Sessions

In contrast, biblical counseling looks like this:

Weeks
Between
Sessions

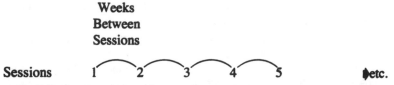

Sessions   1   2   3   4   5   ▶etc.

The high points for counselees engaged in nouthetic change are out there all week long, day after day, as they grapple with their responsibilities in relationship to God and neighbor. The counselee is sent forth to *live* during the week what he is *taught* during the session. Then, his performance, or lack of it, is evaluated at the next session. Thus change happens more quickly and lasts longer because it involves all the elements mentioned in II Timothy 3:16.

Also, usually at the second or third session (you can't do everything during the first session), the counselee is given a copy of the daily devotional workbook *Four Weeks with God and Your Neighbor,* that was designed for use with counselees. This practical guide emphasizes prayer and Bible study that leads to transformed living. Each week the counselor checks up on the work done through this book.

Along the way, assignments that may involve bringing others to a counseling session to settle a problem, going to seek forgiveness of a brother, etc., are regularly given. Many of the significant breakthroughs in a counselee's life occur as the result of such encounters.

Counselors, throughout counseling, stress the counselee's obligation to fulfill God's commandments *whether he feels like it or not.* Excuses are not accepted; reasons are carefully considered in the light of biblical truth. Such reasons often uncover problems not previously understood.

In general, there should be overall progress that may involve peaks and valleys:

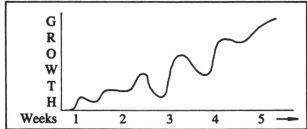

Setbacks, like the ones experienced at weeks 3 and 4, are taken in stride. The counselor carefully examines them to discover what led to them. They are not considered only (or even primarily) in terms of what (at times) may be their tragic side (though that is clearly acknowledged). Rather, since in God's providence they happened, an attempt is made to learn as much as possible from them. Frequently, some of the most vital information of all is gleaned from such an analysis. Thus, in the spirit of Romans 5:20, the counselor endeavors to turn all liabilities into assets. He remembers how God turned a cross into a crown!

Counseling is terminated (1) when the problems presented, along with any others that surfaced along the way, have been dealt with adequately, (2) when the counselee has been restored to usefulness in Christ's church, (3) when he understands the biblical dynamic that freed him from his problem, (4) when he has learned how to avoid future failure and has developed alternative habit patterns to replace sinful ones, (5) when he himself knows what to do to get out of problems in the future, if he should fall into them, (6) when he has learned how to generalize the biblical principles and procedures that he followed in counseling to new and different situations, (7) when he has been restored to his place of usefulness in the local church.

These seven criteria form a rigorous standard of success in counseling, but must be maintained if we wish to help people adequately and to avoid the need for counselees to return again and again.

After the terminating session, there is a routine six-week checkup in which the counselee's unaided progress is evaluated against the seven standards above. When necessary, an additional session or two may be scheduled to solidify or refine one or more areas in the counseiee's life.

Much more could be said about the counseling process, but this thumbnail sketch roughly describes some of the efforts that are typically made.

31

Chapter Seven

TWENTY-FIVE BASIC PRINCIPLES

To try to categorize these 25 biblical counseling principles, and place them in systematic order, is a task that I shall leave for another time, another place and (perhaps) another person. Instead, I shall simply state them and describe them, one by one, without even attempting to give biblical grounds or argumentation for them (I have done the work in my other books). The list isn't exhaustive but does contain a number of useful principles together with a brief explanation of each that may prove helpful for reference.

1. Check out possible organic causes of problems.

While laymen are not supposed to be physicians or diagnosticians, it is important to be aware of the possibility of organic causes of behavioral problems. Whenever there is the slightest suspicion that the difficulty may have organic roots, refer your counselee to a physician (not a psychiatrist) for a medical checkup. In *The Journal of Pastoral Practice*, published quarterly by The Christian Counseling and Educational Foundation, Bob Smith, M.D., has been describing various signs and symptoms, in laymen's language, to help Christian counselors detect such difficulties so that they may know when to refer a counselee to a physician. Be sure you refer to a physician—a man who does *body* work—not a psychiatrist.

2. Don't encourage unrepentant persons to attempt new behavior.

To do so is to encourage failure, hypocrisy and the false assurance that God will settle for something less than true repentance. Repentance is a thorough change of mind that always leads to confession of sin and a desire to change. In all you do, guard against counselees trying to change sinful patterns apart from conviction of sin and repentance.

3. Negotiate agendas to harmonize with the Bible.

Unless the counselee wants what God wants, he will tend to settle for lower priorities. His top priority in counseling always must be to please God in the problem. All else must be secondary to this. Otherwise, changes will tend to be superficial, hypocritical, temporary, and gimmicky. You must warn against ends justifying means.

4. Assign homework after commitment to biblical change.

You invite failure and discouragment if there is no commitment to homework. This commitment, moreover, must be wholehearted and free, not partial or coerced. Be sure, too, that all homework is clear, written, fully explained, and thoroughly understood by the counselee.

5. Collect all relevant data.

It is better to err on the side of thoroughness, if need be, than to miss something vital. That doesn't mean that small, early gains cannot be made' through homework based on data already gained. They can; they *must*. Homework can always be given about *something*. Assignments should be given at the first session to demonstrate that faith must lead to works, that some change is *always* possible and in order to develop the expectation of change from the start.

6. Change takes place in concrete ways.

Change never occurs in the abstract. People are not really "inconsiderate," nor do they become "considerate." They do (or fail to do) things that we label "considerate," "inconsiderate." Homework assignments, therefore, must be concrete ("put your socks in the hamper"), not abstract ("show consideration for your wife this week"). You will discover what homework to assign from gathering specific concrete facts. Ask for lists (e.g., "List a hundred ways in which you have failed as a wife and mother." Few people can come up with 100 abstractions—long lists almost assure concreteness). In data gathering, never settle for generalizations (if they can't be supported by specifics, they probably are wrong): continually say, "Give me an example or six of that, please."

7. Solve problems in proper sequence.

Some difficulties must be handled before others. Failure to recognize this and to place problems in proper order, will lead to an inability to move ahead. An example of this is the necessity for forgiveness *as the basis* for reconciliation and a new relationship. See also, principle no. 8.

8. Deal with both relationships and issues.

Some counselors focus only on issues. Once they have convinced the counselee of the biblical principle or viewpoint, they expect him to change automatically; when he doesn't, they are perplexed. A person may be convinced of God's will but still refuse to change. One reason is relational problems: his attitude toward another person has not yet changed. No matter how fully convinced they may be that they ought to end their separation and return to one another, an estranged husband and wife will not do so until their personal relationship has been dealt with. When getting nowhere on an issue, check attitudes and relationships for possible blocks.

9. Never minimize.

Don't minimize the severity of a counselee's problem (but see principle no. 10 for balance). Nor should you minimize his negative evaluation of himself. It isn't easy for a sinner to admit his sin. Some, meaning well, do poorly instead when they say things like, "O, come on, John, you haven't been that bad of a father." If a wife says "I've been a miserable failure as a mother," take her seriously. Say something like this in response: "That's serious; tell me how bad a mother you have been." Minimize neither the evaluation that the counselee makes, nor the severity of his situation. Rather maximize the Savior: "Yes, your situation is really bad, but—thank God—Jesus Christ can solve problems even that serious."

10. True empathy is deep enough to disagree.

Enter deeply enough into the counselee's problem to discover what it looks like from God's viewpoint (i.e., biblically). You will then see *more* about it than he/she does. This, at times, will lead to *empathetic disagreement*. Unless there is some point at which you disagree with the counselee, you will have no counsel to offer him. Your stance, for instance, ought to be, "No, even though this problem is as bad as it could get [you don't minimize, you see], it isn't impossible. Christ has an answer even to *this*." The point of disagreement is always the point of hope at which counseling can begin.

11. Empathize with suffering, not with self-pity.

There is a difference between the suffering that one must bear and the unnecessary debilitating, self-inflicted and self-induced suffering of self-pity. To empathize with the latter is to encourage sin. Brooding, sulking and fretting are unnecessary. Instead, as I Peter shows, a Christian must trust and obey even in the midst of true suffering. There is enough to suffer in a world cursed by sin; we do not need to add to it by such attitudes.

12. Move as quickly as possible from problem to solution.

Some counselees want only to talk about their problems. But as a counselor, you should be solution-oriented, not problem-oriented. There is no value in morbid introspection or in long, drawn out confessions that border on self-flagellation. Introspection, confession, discussion of the past, all have one purpose—to bring the counselee to a state of intelligent and genuine repentance, that he may quickly resolve his problems God's way. There is no place for punishing the counselee. God wants your counselee to seek forgiveness, right wrongs, live for Him. Your goal, remember, is to *restore* him; there should be no desire to see him grovel in abject misery or in carrying out penance.

13. Watch for attitudes or mind-sets.

These are revealed largely in the counselee's words. Watch out for clichés, key words, etc., that reveal how the counselee thinks. Words like "can't, impossible, hopeless" tell you a good bit. That is the language of despair. Other attitudes involving anger, worry, guilt, resignation, etc., are discovered not only by the choice of words and phrases the counselee uses, but by his pitch, intonation and the body language accompanying them. Clichés, stories, phrases repeated frequently also point to mind-sets. You must challenge these when their thrust runs counter to the Scriptures and inhibits progress in counseling.

14. Look for new developments.

The counselee's life does not stand still from the first session to the last. New factors develop that often influence the counseling situation in one way or another. These can be of great significance. The counselor, from week to week, should inquire about new elements: "Well, has anything I should know about happened since I last saw you?"

15. Remember church discipline.

This process is a right and privilege of every counselee that must not be neglected. Matthew 18:15ff. must be used in certain cases. Lay counselors, in such instances, will find it necessary to engage church officers when, because of open rebellion, etc., counselees (or others involved in their problems) refuse to be reconciled at lower levels.

16. Your own life can influence counseling.

The counselor must continually be upgrading his own life. You will tend to fail to help counselees in areas in which you yourself have weaknesses. Either clear up your own problems, or refer the counselee to another while you are doing so.

17. Doctrinal error may be involved.

Because doctrine affects life, counselees may be in trouble because of faulty teaching, belief, etc. You must know your Bible well enough to discern error. One way to begin is to study *More than Redemption*, a book in which I have related doctrine to counseling.

18. Counselees on drugs require a special approach.

Heavily drugged and drunken persons should not be counseled until they are free from the influence of the drug. You must learn something about drugs so that you will know whether you are talking to a pill or a person in counseling. Whenever drugs interfere, have the counselee tell his physician about the problem and ask him to reduce or eliminate the dosage. Counsel only sober persons.

19. Sleep loss may lead to perceptual problems.

In some persons, sleep loss can lead to all the effects of L.S.D. Don't try to counsel hallucinating persons who haven't been sleeping; put them to bed! Then, after adequate rest, counsel them about any problems that may have led to the loss of sleep. Of course, hallucinations, and other perceptual problems, can stem from a number of other causes.

20. Replace sinful patterns with biblical alternatives.

Change is a two-factored dynamic. Counselees cannot *break* habits, as the world says; they must *replace* them. Your task, then, is not merely to get the counselee to stop certain sinful activities, but to continue to work with him until he has replaced them with righteous patterns. Often counselees will want to terminate counseling *before* this is accomplished; they must be shown the necessity for continuing.

21. Watch your approach.

You must be careful not to inhibit counseling by your personality, actions, words, etc. There is a difference between the offense of the cross and the offense of the counselor. Your approach should be lovingly firm, meek, concerned, helpful. When it is, your personality will not add to the problem but will aid in reaching its solution.

22. Always call sin "sin."

It is no favor to the counselee to call sin "sickness" or "a genetic problem." The kindest thing to do is to tell the truth. There is hope in right labelling. Jesus came to forgive and to defeat sin. He doesn't promise to change our genes or to heal all our sicknesses. Names are important. Names can be signs *and* sign posts: they point to solutions. "Sickness" points to the physician; "sin" points to Jesus Christ.

23. Stress obedience to God, regardless of feeling.

To do what God says, when one does not feel like it isn't hypocrisy; it is simple obedience. I am not a hypocrite if I get out of bed in the morning when I don't feel like it; I am acting responsibly. You must stress that feelings will change when we do what we know God wants us to do—simply to please Him.

24. Stress the counselee's response.

It isn't the wrong that has been done to the counselee that is of such great importance in counseling, but the response that the counselee has learned to make to wrong. Work hard at discovering the counselee's habitual, unbiblical response patterns; it is these that counseling deals with. What others have done is unfortunate—often sad and even tragic—but that can't be changed. How the counselee responds to wrong can be. You also may generate hope by pointing this out. The counselee isn't "stuck" with a lifestyle dictated by others. Greek and Roman converts in N.T. times also had very bad backgrounds, but the Epistles show that God expected them to change their lives *in spite of* their upbringing and their past. God's grace in this is sufficient.

25. Use all the resources of the church.

When a counselee needs a home, there should be a Christian household available. Assign courses taught at church for problems, call on dedicated businessmen, housewives, etc., to assist in working with special problems. There are great, untapped resources in the church that ought to be plugged into counseling.

These 25 principles are by no means exhaustive, but because of their basic nature they may not only teach but provide a quick reference guide to which you may find yourself turning again and again prior to a counseling session. Also, at times when you are stuck, and counseling seems to bog down, a rapid survey of these principles may remind you of something you have neglected that may get counseling on the road again.

Chapter Eight

DISCIPLINE: A TWO-EDGED SWORD

Too many counseling failures are the result of the lack of discipline in the life of a counselor. Most counselees, whatever other problems they may have, in addition, have a problem with undisciplined living. They may not be aware of this as a problem, but the counselor should. Whether or not a counselee states lack of discipline as a contributing or complicating problem, the counselor should look for it in his life. In some counselees, lack of discipline is itself the fundamental difficulty.

The nature of the situation is such that, when problems go unsolved for any length of time, they eat away at whatever structure and discipline one has. Even normally well-disciplined persons may see this happening; when they do, it only aggravates the situation for them. There is a tendency in those whose problems have continued for some time to give up on many responsibilities and interests. Even when this spirit of "what's the use?" doesn't spiral down into serious depression, it can play havoc with whatever life structure remains. Add to this the fact that many (not all) of the persons who need counseling lead rather undisciplined lives anyway and you have all the ingredients for a rather nasty stew. Either way, when they begin counseling, most counselees are in dire need of help in the area of discipline. REMEMBER THIS FACT.

At the very core of the problem of the undisciplined life is lack of structure, and often that results from lack of purpose. The disciplined person knows where God wants him to go and structures his life to take himself there. Moreover, he structures into his life ways of reminding himself of obligations and methods for assuring himself that he will meet them. He plans ahead, makes commitments, sets deadlines, schedules his life, and sticks to his schedule *no matter how he feels*. The undisciplined person rarely does any of these things.

Instead, an undisciplined person gets himself into trouble by following feelings instead of obligations. Since his life structure is minimal, he finds it relatively easy to fall into the feelings trap, has a hard time saying "no," and allows circumstances or other people to run his life. He may set goals but rarely reaches them because he fails to erect those structures that are necessary for attaining them. He avoids making commitments because he knows that he is likely not to keep them. Then, he wonders why he never gets anywhere. He may blame God and others for his failure, but until he is shown the true nature of his difficulty he will never attain his goals.

Now all of this is of the utmost importance to the lay counselor. If he is largely going to be working with people like that, and if it is necessary for him to help counselees to discipline their lives for godliness (I Tim. 4:7), he must know all about discipline. He must be able to suggest ways and means for counselees to discipline their lives, he must plan to regularly monitor their progress to be sure that they meet their responsibilities, and he must do this *in a highly disciplined* manner throughout the course of counseling. The only way to develop new biblical patterns of life is through structure leading to structure. Scriptural analyses and answers, the best intentions in the world and even commitment to biblical goals—though all good and necessary—will fail if these are not a part of an overall structure designed and motivated to produce what God intends. But even that often bogs down unless the counselor encourages, rebukes, demonstrates, explains, praises, etc., all along the way.

When failure occurs because of lack of structure or monitoring, it is almost worse than if no attempt had been made. Counselees then may become discouraged with what they see clearly to be biblical goals and solutions that failed—for lack of discipline! Such discouragment can become the occasion for despair, doubt and defeat. So you must not fail here!

From all of this, you can see that the counselor himself must be disciplined. Discipline is a two-edged sword that cuts both counselor and counselee. The counselor must live a disciplined life to teach disciplined living. In counseling and in his personal life (this carries over into counseling) the counselor must learn to structure life by God's priorities and principles. It works the other way too: doing concerned counseling helps to discipline the counselor.

God planned His work, then worked his plan. Christ's ministry was carried out according to a schedule: He came "in the fullness of time," spoke of the fact that His "hour had not yet come," and died for sinners—right on schedule. Who are we, creatures made in the image of God, to think that we can get along without planning and scheduling?

Discipline and structure (or the lack of it) begins with the way in which counseling is set up. Then, how it is carried on continues to aid or inhibit discipline in the counselee. Most lay counselors think they will see counselees whenever it is convenient. They do not act in a very structured way about counseling itself. Better than this is to say to any potential counselee: "This looks like it is going to take us more than one session. I will meet you here for the next 8-10 weeks at 4 p.m. every Thursday. We will meet regularly, have regular assignments that are to be done on time and, unless there is a truly physical illness, both of us must commit ourselves to being present. Your life is too important to be handled in a slipshod manner."

When a counselee doesn't show up, phone him/her. Ask what happened. If, as so often is true, he says, "I just wasn't feeling up to coming," you should say "That's just when you most need to be here. I'll wait for you—come right over now." Be lovingly firm. Don't accept excuses. Insist that he keep his commitment. Explain that it is this sort of behavior that (at least in part) got him into his difficulties, and that you would be no friend of his if you let him off on such an excuse. Tell him "I won't contribute to your problem." Insist, throughout counseling, that he honor all proper commitments, complete all homework assignments, and accomplish whatever else he ought to be doing. Many counselees know what is wrong and even know what to do; all that they need is someone to help them by riding herd on them. At the end, they will thank you for it, no matter how much they groan along the way.

Go about counseling in a structured way; make everything you do subservient to God's purposes. Spell out to the counselee ahead of time the sorts of things you plan to do in counseling, what kinds of expectations you have, how long counseling might take, pitfalls that you foresee, etc. Use the P.D.I. and the homework book. These structured helps show that you mean business. Explain throughout what you are doing and why (anything you can't explain you ought not to be doing). Anticipate your counselee's questions. Gather data in a systematic way, covering all areas of the counselee's life. Carefully analyze problems, failures, etc., in biblical language and whatever you discover discuss in terms of biblical labels and categories. Don't use psychological jargon.

Give the counselee booklets, like my *Godliness through Discipline*, to emphasize the importance of discipline, to teach him what discipline is, to show him how to structure his life and to encourage him to begin leading a more disciplined life. Discover and list all the areas of his life that lack discipline and determine what must be done to restructure each in a disciplined way.

In everything, however, remember structure is not inflexible. You must never be rigid, insisting on structure for structure's sake. Indeed, it is structure alone that allows for flexibility and change. You cannot change something that isn't there! You only know that you are doing right when you make a change in your schedule, for instance, when you have a well-structured schedule that shows you if there is a possibility for the change. Lack of structure creates chaos.

Change of circumstances may demand revision of a schedule. When school ends in the spring, and the children are home all day, that calls for a schedule different from the one used in the winter when they were in school. Always be willing to change a schedule when it no longer serves its purpose, but never revise a schedule for other reasons. "Follow a schedule, whether you feel like it or not; that's one of the prime reasons you made it in the first place!" That is what you will find yourself telling counselees over and over again.

All these, and many other aspects of discipline that you will discover as you help counselees to structure their lives for godly living are a vital part of effective counseling. As much counseling founders and runs aground on the reefs of undisciplined practices in counseling as for any other reason. Don't let this happen to you.

Chapter Nine

HELP ON DATA GATHERING[1]

An important aspect of counseling is data gathering. The following four helps will be found useful in collecting data. When you know what motivates people to seek counseling, what problems are common to various classes of persons, how to discover where their major known difficulties lie, and how to uncover unknown data, your effectiveness to help counselees will increase greatly. Each of the helps that follow is designed to do each of these things.

Why People Come for Counseling

It is important to distinguish among the various problems that motivate persons to seek help. The following list, while not exhaustive, may aid. It includes twenty of the most frequent reasons why persons seek counselors.

1. Advice in making simple decisions
2. Answers to troublesome questions
3. Depression and guilt
4. Guidance in determining careers
5. Breakdowns
6. Crises
7. Failures
8. Grief
9. Bizarre behavior
10. Anxiety, worry, and fear
11. Other unpleasant feelings
12. Family and marital trouble
13. Help in resolution of conflicts with others
14. Deteriorating interpersonal relations
15. Drug and alcohol problems
16. Sexual difficulties
17. Perceptual distortions
18. Psychosomatic problems
19. Attempted suicide
20. Difficulties at work or school

---

1. From Jay E. Adams, *The Christian Counselor's New Testament* (Grand Rapids: Baker Book House), pp. 703-712.

It is important to know in what areas problems are likely to lie. With various classes of persons, special areas ordinarily (perhaps *usually*) contain the "hot spots."

With *children,* counselors should look for problems in child/parent relations, peer-group difficulties, and teacher and school tensions.

With *older children and singles,* in addition to some of the above, explore the possibility of sexual difficulties, dating problems, communication breakdown, trouble with life-meaning, the discovery, development and use of gifts, and school and/or work.

With *older singles,* look especially for resentment over failure to marry and explore objectionable habit patterns that may have become obstructions to and reduce one's marriage potential. Look for possible homosexual or lesbian problems. Check up on disorganization of life schedules.

With *married persons,* investigate not only strains arising from the marriage itself, but from the family's relationship to in-laws, problems relating to work or homemaking, financial worries, and the discipline of children. Communication breakdown, resentment, and depression are all possibilities too.

Older persons may suffer from loneliness, self-pity, physical aches and pains, time wastage, purposelessness, and fear of death.

Handicapped persons also present specialized problems. In particular, look for resentment (against God and/or others), loneliness, and self-pity. A sense of uselessness may prevail. Such persons need to be shown how to thank God for problems and how to turn their liabilities into assets by the grace of God. Often the handicapped counselee has developed patterns in which he has learned to use his handicap to manipulate others around him.

Not all of these problems are always present in each case. In some instances the special factors that characterize an individual in a particular category may play no part in the problem at all. Yet, even where some other problem or problems not specifically related to age, or singleness, or marriage, etc., seem to dominate, the special problems within the category may form secondary or complicating problems (e.g., "I know why we had the argument; I'm old and useless and just in everyone's way"), and will have to be dealt with as well.

Extensive Questioning

In data gathering, remember to ask *what* type questions rather than *why* type questions. The former are more likely to elicit facts, the latter speculation. In gathering data, if possible, always begin with extensive rather than intensive questioning.

In this approach the counselor uses the shotgun rather than the rifle. He sprays questions like shot across the whole gamut of life. The counselor may wish to open the helps to the following list when doing extensive counseling. Space has been provided for adding one's own additional questions. The list is suggestive, not exhaustive. Ask about:

1. *The counselee's relationship to God;* to the church. Is he saved, is there guilt over particular sins, what are his life goals, have there been any significant changes in these areas lately?

2. *His habits* of Scripture reading and study, prayer, Christian service, use of gifts, witnessing.

3. *His relationship to others:* wife/husband, father/mother, children, in-laws (especially the wife's mother-in-law or a daughter-in-law), neighbors, relatives, other significant persons.

4. *His work (or school work):* does he enjoy it, have problems with it, is he

afraid of failure, does he do an adequate job? What about his relationship to others? Any recent changes at work?

5. *His physical life:* adequate exercise, sleep (remember the effects of significant sleep loss), and diet; about illnesses, injuries, or bodily abuses. What about the sexual life?

6. *His financial affairs:* does he tithe and give to the church, pay bills, budget the funds, pay taxes faithfully? Does his/her spouse and he/she argue over money? Any recent financial setbacks?

7. *Social and recreational.* Adequate? Family, husband/wife outings, vacations, dates, friends?

8. *Time:* organized, disorganized? Priorities right before God? Schedule? Behind?

9. Have there been any *tragedies, deaths, crises, major life changes recently,* in last half year, in last year?

10. Is there *fear, anger, bitterness and resentment, depression, guilt* or other bad feelings, attitudes?

These questions are supplemental to those asked on the Personal Data Inventory, and are not intended to replace them. Some are repetitious, but it is often necessary to ask a question more than once in different contexts.

As the counselor checks out these areas, he makes a careful record of responses (recording both core and halo data), asking further questions that grow out of feedback, but never allowing the checkout to become bogged down in any one area. In the agenda column, the counselor makes notations of all the areas that he will want to investigate more intensively later on. These include areas in which core data indicate certain or possible problems and where halo data (nervousness, body movements, unusual tension, stuttering, surprise, embarrassment, regret, evasion, etc.) seem to indicate particular sensitivity.

Discovering Problem Patterns

Patterns are not always known to the counselee and may not immediately become apparent to the counselor. The use of a D.P.P. Form may be assigned as homework for one to four weeks to help uncover such patterns. The form has been designed for simplicity of use by the counselee. A sample follows:

Name ....

Date ....

Directions: For one week carefully list *all* events, situations or activities (good or bad) that resulted in _____ .
Circle those that occur three or more times.

	Sun.	Mon.	Tues.	Wed.	Thur.	Fri.	Sat.
Morning							
Afternoon							
Evening							

The D.P.P. is a flexible instrument. For instance, if a counselee is concerned about breaking a pattern of eating between meals, he may keep a

D.P.P. to determine when he eats (or desires to). He may discover from this that eating is connected with certain situations such as (1) when watching TV, (2) when concerned about the children, (3) when under stress, (4) just before supper when hungry. Gathering such data is useful for mapping out a strategy for breaking and replacing the habit. In interpreting the D.P.P., look for recurring events (situations) or periods (time). The pattern may be geographical, chronological, interpersonal, etc. The form is available in the *Christian Counselor's Starter Packet* or in any quantity from the publisher.

Question Asking

I. Begin with the three basics (all *what* type questions).

These are a summary of the questions asked by Christ and the apostles.

A. Q. 1.—What is your problem? (Three levels of responses).

1. Irritation level—"I'm depressed."
2. Particular instance—"I'm depressed because I had a brawl with my mother-in-law."
3. Underlying pattern—"I'm depressed because I had a brawl like I always do when I lose my cool."

B. Q. 2.—What have you done about it?

1. Further complicated matters in the attempts to solve it.
2. Failed to realize that other matters are even more serious (e.g., the *relationship* must be healed before the solution to the *issue* is possible).

C. Q. 3.—What do you want me to do?

1. Agenda problem—be sure that you both want the same thing: God's will.
2. Basic motivation to please God (not to get wife back, get relief from the misery, etc.; all else is secondary).

II. Seek data

A. Stress *what* type questions (to elicit facts) rather than *why* type questions (that evoke speculation).

B. Do not ask questions that can be answered by yes/no. (Save those for commitment).

C. Let subsequent questions grow from previous answers.

1. As in normal conversations.
2. With this exception: you have been invited to ask more personal questions (but there are still limits).

D. Ask questions from extensive and intensive approaches.

E. Watch for nonverbal halo data.

F. Ask for exact, concrete specifics; do not settle for generalizations or abstractions.

Listening

There is much misinformation about the value and the place of listening in counseling. While listening is a vital aspect of counseling, remember that it is only one aspect. It must never be equated with counseling as if it were the all-in-all or even the most important aspect of the work. Listening is *one* essential means to the counselor's ends.

I. God says: Listen for *facts* (Prov. 18:13).
   A. Don't jump to conclusions (e.g., appearances deceive).
      1. The first problem raised may not be the most basic one.
      2. It may have been offered as a trial balloon to see how you handle problems.
   B. One reason for the failure suggested: the counselor may be too anxious to speak.
      1. He may offer a few pat answers (solutions) for everything, or his problem may be
      2. Stereotyping (failure to recognize true diversity), or
      3. Failure to distinguish things that differ but look alike:
         a. Bizarre behavior from sleep loss; from organic causes.
         b. Tendency to identify with a recent success: "Looks just like the case I handled last week," or
      4. Failure to distinguish the three levels of response to the question, "What is your problem?"
   C. You need to gather facts:
      1. God doesn't stress the value of listening per se in this passage,
      2. But the value of listening as a means for obtaining data about which to speak.
      3. Verse 13 (and 15) pictures a data-gatering situation.
   D. The passage does not imply that no response, no advice will be given, but rather
      1. That, contrary to Carl Rogers,
      2. Listening is to gather data that will enable one to answer and advise properly.
      3. These verses are not problem-focused, but solution-oriented.

II. Listen *actively* for the facts (Prov. 18:5).

A. The listener is pictured not passively but actively listening
   1. To *acquire* knowledge,
   2. By *seeking* it.
B. The data needed to give an appropriate answer do not come from listening
   1. To stream-of-consciousness talk structured by the counselee,
   2. But to talk elicited by and structured by the counselor.
C. The counselor must control the flow of talk.
   1. He seeks and finds data he is looking for as well as those data that the counselee wishes to offer.
   2. He is prudent and wise in the way in which he conducts the data-gathering sessions.
      a. He knows what to ask,
      b. When to ask it,
      c. And how to word his questions (see material on question asking).
D. He listens for facts, not merely for attitudes and feelings.
   1. Notice, he seeks "knowledge" or "information."
   2. Notice further, feeling is not once mentioned in these verses.
III. Listen for *all* of the facts (Prov. 18:17).
   A. There are two or more sides to many issues:
      1. This implies that all parties should be present if possible,
      2. That each should hear what the other party says in order to explain, modify, amplify, etc. (note "examine"),
      3. And it is clear that one must not be allowed to speak negatively about another behind his back (see also James 4:11).
   B. The first to speak can sound quite convincing if heard alone,
      1. But the additional information that the other provides can turn the conclusion about face.
      2. As, for instance, when one counselee said, "He hit me! He slapped me in the face!"
      And her husband replied:
      "Sure, to bring her to her senses. She was hysterically screaming and beating herself on the head with her fists."

Chapter Ten

A BIBLICAL ANALYSIS OF THE PROBLEM

I have mentioned already the great importance of biblical language and categories, pointing out that terms are not only signs of things signified but also sign*posts* that point to solutions of problems. The categories that we use to classify data also are of importance since they prejudice, direct and limit thought. Let me explain that just a bit. Some personality tests have a category that searches for "latent homosexuality." The existence of that category presupposes that homosexuality is genetic. Given the acceptance and use of the test, the counselor's thinking is set in a particular direction. On the contrary, in biblical thought one would classify homosexuality as a life-dominating sin.

The call for a biblical analysis, including both biblical language and categories, grows out of the presuppositions or assumptions that

1. biblical terminc'ogy and thought is more accurate;
2. the Bible can be wholly trusted.

But what else is involved in a biblical analysis of a counselee's problem? Perhaps the best way to answer that question, and to set everything in its proper perspective is to take a case and discuss it. For this purpose, I shall use Case Number 20, page 40 in *The Christian Counselor's Casebook.*

"MY LIFE IS A BIG FAT ZERO"

Midge is a 23-year-old, single working girl. She is a graduate of a Bible college and now works as a secretary at the same school.

On the Personal Data Inventory she describes herself as being "often—blue," "shy," and "lonely." She also adds: "I'm a no-thing," and "I feel inferior." She says that she prays often but reads her Bible only occasionally.

As she sees it, this is the main problem: "My self concept is just absolutely zero. That may surprise you, but it is. My whole life has been a big, fat zero. Nobody notices me, nobody likes me, and nobody cares about me. I may as well be dead. I feel so inadequate. Even when I pray I can't find any relief. Probably the Lord doesn't even like me. But he is the one who made me this way, so maybe he does."

Most modern counselors would say that Midge has a problem with "self-image." Her "self-concept," they would hasten to add, is poor and she needs "ego-enhancing." She must be helped to acquire a sense of "self-worth"; that sort of thing then becomes the major task of counseling. If we were to analyze her past we'd probably discover that in one way or another she has been put down continually. That will be thought to be the cause of her problem. That is the assessment of the case that you'd hear from many today. But the analysis is faulty and will point in the wrong direction. The fact that others who have been demeaned by parents or peers did *not* develop similar problems will be ignored. And, that Midge's attitude may have involved much of this will not be considered.

The words in quotation marks in the last paragraph actually structure for us a non-biblical analysis of Midge's problem. They do not really help; instead they limit and direct one's thinking into the wrong channels. Nor are these channels hopeful. We know there is no way to bolster or pump up her image of herself. Some, following Adler, would focus on her comments "I feel inferior, I feel so inadequate," and say that she has an inferiority complex.

But as a biblical counselor you will avoid all such analyses. Midge herself has already bought the Maslow-Adler line (especially the former) and analyzes herself *in terms* of self-image and inferiority. Her own thinking and responses to life have been shaped, limited and conditioned by the construct this eclectic view of things presupposes and, indeed, demands. That means that as her counselor you will have to help her to see the problem differently. You must help her to open her thinking to new, biblical concepts.

Notice, also, that with Maslow (who provides the excuse) Midge explains that since others have not satisfied her basic needs by loving, liking and caring for her she is incapable of making it in life. The categories that one accepts will structure his analysis of the problem. Midge depends largely on self-image notions in analyzing her situation; and it is clear that the acceptance of the categories leading to that analysis has done her little good. She may not know much about Maslow or self-image views, but, like so many, she has picked up ideas here and there which are generally abroad in the culture.

Now, how would a Christian view Midge's problem? Since the Bible nowhere tells us that we cannot obey God or solve problems unless our needs have been met by others, and because in the Bible God treats all of His children alike, giving them the same commands and holding before them the same standards, regardless of whether they were raised in a pious Hebrew family, knowing the Scriptures from childhood and worshiping the true God Jehovah, or they were pagan Corinthians who were involved in idolatry, temple prostitution, lying, etc., we will analyze Midge's problem quite differently. Our Christian categories demand a different outcome; one that is more hopeful because it is God's.

First, we must take her seriously when she says "I'm a nothing" and "My whole life has been a big fat zero." We will want to respond with words something like this: "That's serious; to waste a life that God has given that way is a tragedy. You must have some pretty good reasons for reaching such a drastic conclusion. Tell me some of the ways in which you have failed." Those statements, in accordance with I Corinthians 13:7, "love . . . believes all things," place the responsibility for her problem just where it belongs—on her. We must take her seriously about her negative evaluation of herself.

But there are some other statements of hers that we must counter. They are not statements of fact, such as those that we have accepted, but statements of value, particularly those that demonstrate by language and orientation, an incorrect, unbiblical interpretation of these facts. The string of Maslow/ Adler interpretations of her plight must be rejected. To do so is crucial; there is no other way to (1) rightly analyze the situation, (2) honor God and (3) give her hope and direction that will enable her to do something about her problem.

Moreover, we shall want to correct her statements about *feeling* inferior and inadequate, pointing out to her that neither inferiority nor inadequacy is a feeling. One simply doesn't *feel* inferior or inadequate. Doubtless she feels lousy, but that isn't because either of these factors is a feeling. She feels *bad* because she has *judged* herself to *be* inferior and inadequate. The bad feelings she has were occasioned by her judgment about the facts.

Viewing the matter this way, we may ask "Is her judgment about herself correct or incorrect?" And we can help her to reexamine and reassess the facts on which that judgment is based. If inferiority or inadequacy were feelings we could do nothing about them. There is no way that a counselor could get her to change such "feelings." Let me take one of her judgments and run it through such an analysis:

Judgment: "I am inadequate."

If a careful reassessment of the evidence does not support this conclusion, she must admit that she is wrong. Such an analysis will eliminate the bad feelings that the false judgment triggered.

If it is right not to be inadequate in some way or other (it would be right to be inadequate in the ring with Muhammed Ali), then, on acceptance of this fact, bad feelings from guilt should disappear. Other bad feelings from disappointment, regret, etc., may linger for a brief time but should not debilitate unless they grow out of anger and pride that makes her want to be able to do anyway what God has not gifted her to do.

If a careful reassessment of the evidence supports Midge's conclusion, she must then decide what to do about it. Her next step is to ask "Is it or isn't it right before God for me to be inadequate in the ways that I am?"

If it is wrong (for instance, she may have gifts she ought to be using but isn't), then, the counselor may help her to lay out a plan for developing and deploying those gifts. As she begins to do so out of a commitment to God, her bad feelings will lift.

Moreover, when we read her language of exaggeration ("nobody . . . nobody"), her blameshifting (even expressing it toward God), her resentment toward others and her self-pity and self-centeredness, we discover where some of her real problems lie. She doesn't have problems because of a bad self-concept; she has a poor self-concept because of her sinful, unrepentant patterns of life and the unresolved difficulties they have occasioned. Her problem is neither a bad self-concept nor bad treatment by others. Rather, it is a bad self (that she knows is bad) and bad treatment of others (that is clear from her resentful attitudes toward them) that is her major difficulty. She has the biblical principle turned around: instead of losing herself for Christ and His gospel, she is seeking self-gratification. It will never come that way; satisfaction is a by-product and cannot be sought and found directly. No wonder she is miserable—she has never learned that "it is more blessed to give than to receive." She thinks "If people would only be better to me, then I'd be better." She is wrong. Doubtless, many people may have wronged her; but that isn't her problem. Her difficulty lies in the wrong way that she has responded to wrong done to her.

Possibly also, she is concerned that she is yet single though a graduate of a Christian college. She may be angry with God for not providing a husband. But her whole approach to problems is calculated to drive men away rather than to attract them. She needs to be told to stop blaming others and look at herself—that's where the responsibility for change really lies. Why would she consider herself (as she now is) a good risk for marriage?

The Christian analysis is honest, forthright and hard (one might even think severe). But it is accurate, and that is why it is calculated to give hope, to produce change through repentance and to lead to a new life style. The present Maslow/Adler self-concept stance that Midge has taken, though in line with many pagan analyses, will do just the opposite. Midge's problem is sin, and she must be told so. Words like "self-concept," etc., only cloud the issues, create excuses for sin and orient one's thinking in the wrong direction. Midge needs truth.

Chapter Eleven

FINDING THE BIBLICAL SOLUTION

Some counselors are better at analyzing a counselee's problems than they are at discovering the Bible's solution to it or in implementing that solution in a biblical way when the solution has been reached. But it is imperative for lay counselors to become adept in all of these endeavors. One leaves his counselee in a sorry plight if he can accurately tell him all about his dilemma in scriptural language and according to biblical categories, but can do little to help him get out of it. The third and fourth steps of change mentioned in II Timothy 3:16 have to do with getting out and staying out of sinful lifestyles and practices. Since the Bible is adequate for achieving these two ends, you must learn how to use it in a practical way for just such purposes.

First of all, as I have just noted, the biblical solution to a problem is twofold: it consists of

1. getting out of his difficulties with God and with his neighbor,

and

2. teaching him how to stay out of them in the future.

The first one of these objectives has to do with the confession of sin and forgiveness, while the second pertains to the put on/put off dynamic mentioned previously.

Confession

Confession is essentially *agreement*. The N.T. Greek word means "to say the same thing." The word was used in contracts and in other legal documents to mean "agreement." Parties reach an *agreement* which they record and label as such. Confession is agreement with God about one's sin. It is a formal acknowledgment in prayer that God is right in holding us guilty for sin. It is an on-the-record admission of guilt. The confessor says "I have sinned; I acknowledge my transgression." When a counselee sees and is willing and able to articulate his problem in biblical terms and categories, he is then (and only then) in a position where he can *confess* his sin. No other analysis leads him to recognize his attitudes and behavior as sin. Whether he does so or not is, of course, another matter. Continued refusal to confess sin as God directs in Proverbs 28:13, leads at length to failure and misery (God says such a person "won't prosper"—the Hebrew word translated "prosper" means to "succeed, make it through, reach a goal.") and ultimately to the use of church discipline as we have seen already. But for those who do confess we see that confession to God issues in forgiveness by Him (cf. Ps. 32:5).

Forgiveness

Some wonder why we need forgiveness when we have already been forgiven in Christ. The answer is clear: the forgiveness that we received when we first believed in Jesus was judicial; God forgave *as Judge*. Forgiveness after forgiveness—the forgiveness that we are now discussing—is different; it isn't judicial but *fatherly*. Note especially the use of the word Father in relationship to forgiveness in Matthew 6:9-15; I John 1:2, 3, 9. Christians need to confess sins to their heavenly Father and receive His *fatherly* forgiveness. In just the same way, they must confess sin to any others that they have wronged and seek their forgiveness. Then, reconciliation is possible and must be pursued until a new relationship is developed.

Change

But Proverbs 28:13 makes it clear that genuine confession leads to forsaking the sin that has been confessed. Only then can one expect God's blessing. Confession is the acknowledgment of wrong; forsaking involves the put off/put on dynamic. It might seem at first that "forsaking" would correspond only to the "put off" aspect of that dynamic, but the fact of the matter is that no sinful habit has been truly put off until it has been *replaced* by its biblical alternative (Eph. 4:22-24). That is why Paul commands not only that lying be put off, but also that truth be put on in its place (Eph. 4:25), not only that stealing be stopped but that it be replaced with hard work and with giving to those who have genuine need (Eph. 4:28). And so it goes.

Radical Amputation

But in order to put off, one must structure *against* the return of the sinful pattern as well as *for* the furtherance of the righteous one. That is why Christ called us to what I have described as *Radical Amputation*. In Matthew 5:27-30 we read:

"You have heard that it was said, 'You shall not commit adultery.' But I tell you that whoever looks at a woman with the intention of desiring her already has committed adultery with her in his heart. So if your right eye causes you to stumble, tear it out and throw it away from you; it is to your advantage to have one of your members perish than for your whole body to be thrown into Gehenna. And if your right hand causes you to stumble, cut it off and throw it away from you; it is to your advantage to have one of your members perish than for your whole body to gc away into Gehenna."

We must make it clear to the counselee that in this passage Jesus is telling us that:

1. There will be future temptations to repeat past acts of sin. We must be aware of this and guard against them;
2. We must be prepared to meet and defeat such temptations when they come;
3. Nothing may be spared in the process: it is *radical*. Even the *right* eye, the *right* foot or the *right* hand must be sacrificed if necessary in this metaphor. To guard against temptation will cost. It will be as costly as losing a vital part of the body. It will cost labor, may cost associations (I Cor. 15:33), etc. Counselors do counselees a disservice when they fail to tell counselees about this and (consequently) do not call them to count the cost;
4. We must do whatever is required, even to go to the greatest lengths, to make it *very* difficult to sin the same way again;
5. Whatever we do also must make us *aware* of the temptation when it occurs so that we will not unconsciously slip into the sin again without realizing it (to hobble over to commit sin with an amputated foot would do the trick, you see. Of course, Jesus isn't advocating *literal* amputation. What Christ refers to is doing something that may be even as radical to prevent future sin).

The counselor must help the counselee to think of ways and means of erecting obstacles to prevent the repetition of sin. These will differ in each case so that to fulfil Christ's command the counselor and counselee will have to use some thought and (at times) even creativity. It is right there that many counselees come up short; counselors must not. Rather, every lay counselor

59

must develop his ability to see needs and possibilities in the circumstances that will help his counselees to plan against future failure. Christ was concerned about preventing future sin; counselors, ministering in His name also must show such concern.

Let us examine a case to see what sort of things may be done. Bill has been involved in pornography. He repents of his sin. Now, what does he do to guard against yielding to the temptation in the future? There are many possibilities according to the particulars in his individual situation, but here are a few ideas that might enter into the preventive structure that a counselor might wish to build:

1. Bill will throw away *all* pornographic material immediately.
2. He will disassociate himself from all of those persons whom he knows use such materials and with whom he previously swapped them. Telling them of his repentance and witnessing to them about Jesus Christ will, in most cases, effectively bring about the break if it does not lead to conversions. If he protests, explain I Corinthians 15:33.
3. Bill will reroute his daily walk from the commuter train to his place of employment so that he will not pass by the store from which he has been in the habit of purchasing pornographic materials.
4. He will draw up a Philippians 4:8 think list and carry it with him at all times. On the list will be subjects that fit the criteria in Philippians 4:8. When his mind begins to wander to forbidden areas, he will whip out his think list and start concentrating on the next item on the list instead. In this way he will begin to get a leash on his mind and train it to walk in the paths of righteousness rather than let it go roaming all over the neighborhood rummaging into any old garbage pail it can find. Philippians 4:8 is God's leash law for the mind.

There may be any number of other factors that might be included in Bill's structure against sin (clearly, in each case the particulars, and the number of precautions taken will differ with the variables), but these four give *some* indication of the sorts of things that one who is involved in the process of radical amputation will find it necessary to do.

Of course, as I have said earlier, it will not be adequate merely to put off the old sinful pattern. Bill must also work on a new, more satisfactory sexual relationship with his wife, in which he emphasizes what he can give, not what he can get out of sexual relations (cf. I Cor. 7:4). In sex, as elsewhere, he will discover that it is more blessed to give than to receive. This, in part, is the put on that must replace the put off.

Since I already have discussed the put on dimension to some extent, let me make just a couple more suggestions:

1. I suggest that you write out every sinful pattern that you encounter in your life, in the lives of others, and in the Bible's accounts of them. Write each out in biblical terminology, presupposing biblical thought categories in all you do.
2. Then, next to the problem, as you find them, write out the biblical alternatives to these sinful patterns together with the principal scriptural references that appertain to them.

Now, that raises another matter: How does one find the appropriate Scripture to use when presented a sinful life pattern that must be countered? Fundamentally, he must know beforehand most of the principal passages, *together with their meanings* (this understanding comes only from regular, intensive, prayerful study), that refer to the principal problems seen again and again in counseling. That means *preparation*. But prepared as he may be, new situations (or new forms of old ones) will arise that will drive the counselor back to his Bible for additional study. Often when we tend to become over confident, God throws us a curve.

In Appendix B, I have listed a number of counseling subjects, together with some key Scripture passages that, in one way or another, deal with them. I have left ample space for adding other passages. I strongly suggest that you make it your regular practice to study these passages, one by one, using commentaries and other Bible helps, to become thoroughly knowledgable about them. Keep records of the conclusions you reach in your studies, together with notes on ways of using those passages in counseling.

While the solution itself is important, it will get you nowhere unless it is *implemented*. In the next chapter we will consider that question.

Chapter Twelve

IMPLEMENTING A BIBLICAL PLAN

Conservative churches have been strong on discovering what is wrong and even in declaring what ought to be done about it. But they have been extremely weak in telling and showing people *how* to do it. Instead, we (rightly) bring people to conviction of sin and to a commitment to change, only to forsake them at that point. That is tragic, and it accounts for much of the failure and apathy that we see in individual lives and in the corporate life of congregations. Moreover, much counseling founders at this point. This chapter, though only suggestive, is of great importance.

The weakness of which I speak is a problem on several fronts. The same difficulty that we find in counseling occurs just as frequently in preaching. No wonder so many otherwise fine, accurate, even meaty sermons fall like seed on stony ground. Nothing, or at best, very little comes of them, when they are so full of promise. We wonder why! So much time and effort is expended for such meagre returns. It is truly a great waste.

While there are many causes for failure, I am convinced that one prime factor is the lack of *how-to* instruction in sermons and in counseling sessions. When counselors (as well as preachers) wake up to this need and begin to meet it they will see dramatic change in the results that they get for their efforts. Again and again I have seen apathetic counselees come alive at the mere suggestion of ways and means of implementing biblical principles and practices.

Let us consider one factor in a typical case, taken again from the *Christian Counselor's Casebook;* Case Number 11, page 22:

WHY BE DEPRESSED?—YOU'RE A CHRISTIAN

"So the main problem you'd like help with is depression," says the counselor. "We'll see what we can do about it, Jim."

"Good, I'm hoping to find some relief soon," responds the college sophomore.

"First of all, Jim, do you know Jesus Christ as your own personal Savior?"

"Yes I do, Sir. I've been a Christian since I was a young child."

"So you've trusted in Him for forgiveness of sins, and you know that God is your Father?"

"Yes, that's right."

"Well then, as a child of God, it's important for you to know and meditate on the promises of God. Have you ever memorized Scripture?"

"I guess I know a lot of familiar verses by heart, but I've never conducted a conscientious program of memorization."

"Well, I'd like you to do just that. Philippians 4:4 says, 'Rejoice in the Lord always, again I say rejoice.' When you start to get depressed remind yourself of this verse. As a Christain you have plenty to be joyful about."

It should be clear from the record that the counselor in the case does not know what to do. He is concerned about Jim's salvation, and that is good. He utters truths about knowledge of and meditation of the Scriptures, and that is fine. Moreoever, he is correct in saying that a Christian shouldn't be depressed but should rejoice. All this is true. But apart from specific, how-to direction, it becomes mere truism. How does one who is depressed throw off depression? How does he learn to rejoice instead? And how does one meditate, anyway? All these, and a host of similar questions, have been left hanging; the pastor has made no attempt to explain any of this for Jim. Clearly, the pastor, though well meaning, has set Jim up for a fall. He had told him what he ought to do, but his abstract direction and exhortation won't help. Jim needs specific direction, not only concerning what to do—he probably knows much of that anyway—but also concerning how to go about doing it. The counselor has failed him.

Forgetting the facts of the specific case above, but keying on the exhortation about meditation, let me make some observations. The pastor assumes understanding on the counselee's part that very likely he doesn't possess. How many Christians have any substantive idea about what meditation is? If meditation is useful for Jim (or anyone else in counseling) then the pastor ought to take the time to explain

(1) What meditation is;

(2) How it relates to the problem (depression or whatever);

(3) How to meditate (in detail).

Since this is rarely done, it might be of importance to sketch an idea or two on the subject. Moreover, meditation itself, as we shall see, is intimately connected with the "how to" about which I have been speaking.

To begin with, he would want to distinguish biblical meditation from T.M. (transcendental meditation) and other similar forms of meditation practiced and promoted today. These focus one's attention on himself. The Christian, in contrast, meditates on biblical truth. He focuses his attention on Christ and His teaching. Christian meditation is not a trance; it is thought—deep thought—about truth, its implications, and its implementation. Christian meditation involves rational thinking about content.

The two principal words for *meditation* in the Bible mean "to murmur or mutter" and "to speak to one's self." Meditation is a process of thinking (not feeling) through language that takes place in the heart (or inner life). In meditation, a Christian discusses various biblical facts with himself *in an intensive way*. The italicized words at the end of the previous sentence are significant. Sometimes we talk things over with ourselves and quickly come to a decision. That isn't meditation. Meditation is careful, detailed thought that gives the fullest possible consideration to what one is thinking about. And, as I have noted, this all goes on in the heart (Ps. 19:14; 49:3; Isa. 33:18), which is the inner person (I Pet. 3:4) who lives, thinks, speaks (Ps. 14:1) to himself before God (I Sam. 16:7).

Moreover, as one of the Hebrew terms for meditation (the OT was written in Hebrew) indicates, meditation refers to self-talk *that is productive*. This inner meditation on the Scriptures is like a tree with inner resources that cause it to bud, and at length to blossom. So the purpose of meditation is to produce various outer life responses (Josh. 1:8; Prov. 15:28). A Christian meditates, not to attain peace, calmness or a sense of tranquility, as so many wrongly seem to think. Meditation, indeed, may at times be quite upsetting (Isa. 33:18). Meditation is not feeling-oriented; it is a process of focused, concentrated inner reasoning that leads to outer action. As God told Joshua (Josh. 1:8), success in fulfilling God's law depends upon it. The process itself is of no merit or value, nor does it seek to accomplish something subjective for the person meditating. No, it is an inner experience, but one that is designed to achieve objective results. What are these results?

The meditator, as Joshua 1:8 makes clear, wants to understand how to relate biblical truth to life. He will not settle for mere Bible reading, rote memorizing or filing away facts. His burning desire is to turn a truth over and over, and over again, until he knows all he can possibly know about it. He examines it from every vantage point, intently, as one views the many-hued refractions of light that glance off every facet of a diamond. He will not let a truth go until it blesses him! He wants to know that truth in all its length and breadth in his own life. He is not satisfied merely to intellectualize about scriptural data; he thinks through all of its implications and studies ways to implement it. He takes time to plan out ways and means of gearing it into daily living. Meditation is a process of deepening the understanding and of planning.

Curiously, the pastor suggested meditation, but probably had little understanding of what it is. Meditation is what both Jim and the pastor needed. But since the pastor himself was weak on the point (seminarians, unfortunately, don't have courses on meditation) he could not tell Jim *how* to meditate.

Meditation, then, is one way (perhaps the principal way) of coming up with practical, how-to suggestions for implementing truth.

How does one meditate? He *thinks*—during the day, in bed at night and at twilight, during regular times set aside for thought (Ps. 1; Gen. 24:63). He takes a relevant portion of the Scriptures and, having studied its grammatical-historical meaning, then begins to ask:

What does it mean to me?

How will it change my life?

What are some concrete things that I must do about it?

How can I get these things accomplished?

And he does this, as we noted before, *until he produces*. Ideas come, thoughts pour over the rim, plans begin to jell and desire to get on with doing what the Bible requires wells up within. It is not enough to do fine exegetical and doctrinal studies of the Bible, as important as these are for every lay counselor as well as his pastor, he must learn *how* to think about *how to*. Until a counselor, himself, learns the secrets of meditation, he will never be able to instruct others in counseling. That was Jim's pastor's problem.

Planning

When a counselor discovers the problem that a counselee is facing, finds the biblical solution to it, and then helps him to meditate on ways to integrate and implement that solution in his life, what he does usually all comes together in terms of a plan. Rarely can problems be solved or solutions implemented apart from a plan. God plans and schedules His work, as all of the prophecies clearly show; who are we—created in His image—to think that we can get away with doing less?

Any such plan will probably contain at least the following elements:

1. The biblical goal, or goals, to be reached will be detailed, understood and

clearly articulated (often in writing) by both the counselor and the counselee. They will agree that they agree about them, the counselee will express his desire to reach these goals and will commit himself to do so by God's help (grace). Until this is done, counseling will bog down; it will not get past the stage of intellectualizing about the problem. Without clearcut, biblical goals, no commitment can, or should, be made. Too often counselors will settle for foggy, half-understood, partly-agreed-on goals. To do so is to court failure and disappointment. Of course, the ultimate goal in all of this is to honor God. Presumably, this goal was discussed with the counselee under agenda.

2. The goals should be divided into long and short term objectives. The former are those goals in counseling which, when attained, lead to the termination of counseling. The latter are those goals that become essential steps in the process of realizing the long-term goals.

A counseling goal may be a marriage pleasing to God. A long-range goal may be sexual agreement and functioning that is biblical and satisfying. A short-range goal may be learning to satisfy one's partner in foreplay. Short-term goals are mile markers by which progress, or the lack of it, may be gauged.

3. Implementation must always be built into a plan. Otherwise, it is like a beautiful automobile without an engine. Here is where so many go wrong. This implementation will include:

a. scheduling—specific days and/or hours will be agreed on and matters will be scheduled in sequence according to present capacity and priorities;

b. ways and means—detailed, concrete;

c. techniques—known, and, when necessary, practiced;

d. steps and procedures—spelled out clearly.

Now, let's consider an example. Bill and Barb have separated. They seek counseling. The counseling goal is to rebuild their marriage on a sound Christian foundation. Long-range goals will include such times as the establishment of good communication on a biblical basis. Here are some short-term goals that will lead to assigned homework at the first session. These goals will pertain to the following week:

1. Reconciliation through the confession of sin and the granting of forgiveness: to be done immediately, since both are repentant.

2. Bill to return home: immediately after reconciliation.

3. Then, Bill and Barb to make his-and-her lists containing at least 100 items each. These lists are to indicate all the ways that they are failing God and one another as persons, as husband/wife and as parents. The items are to be concrete, specific and not abstract. Each is to read over the other's list *without comment or discussion*. Lists are to be brought to the next counseling session. Here is the very beginning of communicating.
4. Rather than to try to solve problems that arise this week (they have not yet developed this capability) they are to write out any problems in detail and bring them to the next counseling session for discussion.

The four items above are samples of the sort of things that might be done. Note: each is spelled out clearly; times are scheduled, sequences are marked out and failure and dissention are foreseen and guarded against. Temporary measures are adopted where there is lack of capacity. Each session thereafter will require similar planning.

Planning must be flexible, not rigid. But it must not be so flexible that it virtually does not exist. Tentative plans for session number 2 may have to be scrapped if, for example, Barb refused to allow Bill to return home during the week. A new set of short-term goals, concentrating on that issue in detail, might then be necessary. In that way, it is sometimes necessary to take one step backwards to enable counseling eventually to go forward again.

Commitment

All along the way, there will be places in which planning will involve commitment. Until all parties involved are thoroughly committed to a given solution and to the plan by which it is to be attained, failure is inevitable. Commitment involves:
1. A complete and accurate understanding of *all* the details of both the long and short-range goals (including all how-to processes and procedures);
2. A desire to reach all goals in order to please Jesus Christ;
3. Prayer: asking God to supply the wisdom and strength that is needed.

Let me conclude by urging you to take the time required for implementation. It does take time. But in the long run it will be time (and agony) saved.

Chapter Thirteen

FOLLOW THROUGH: WORKING THE PLAN

So far, I have spoken about making a biblical analysis of the problem, finding a biblical solution and implementing a biblical plan of action that incorporates it. Now I shall turn to the matter of *follow through*.

When a golfer swings his club or a pitcher throws a baseball, he sets in motion a course of action that includes not only preparation and delivery but also a follow through. Similarly, when the ball has left the counselee's hand, neither he nor the counselor has really completed his moves.

Follow *through* isn't the same as follow *up*. Follow up involves checking out the counselee's progress. Follow through has to do not only with the *counselee* activity, but also with continued *counselor* activity throughout the period after delivery. Follow through includes, but is greater in scope than, follow up activity.

It is good to explain, important to plan and essential to develop ways and means for implementing a plan, but unless the counselor follows through to the point of successful conclusion (i.e., successful according to biblical standards), in a few months (or weeks) the counselee may be back for counseling again. Or, what is worse, the counselee may become discouraged and give up.

What is this follow through and what does it involve? Follow through can be summarized in two statements:

1. Follow through involves supervision;
2. Follow through involves teaching and training.

I shall turn first to

Supervising

Under the term monitoring, I have mentioned the idea of supervision earlier in this book. Here I wish to enlarge on the question just a bit. Of great significance to counseling are David's words in Psalm 32:8:

> I will instruct you and train you in the way you shall go; I will counsel you with my eye on you (Berkeley).

Summed up in those words is all that I want to say in this chapter about follow through. Immediately, you will see in David's words both of the elements that constitute follow through: supervision and instruction.

First, let's focus on supervision: i.e., counseling another *with one's eye on him*. The phrase used here is similar to ours: "I'm going to keep my eye on you." Indeed, our expression may go back to this source. The idea in the verse has to do with someone giving directions to another and then keeping his eye on him by *watching* to see (1) if he really follows them, (2) if he follows them correctly, (3) if he follows them well and (4) if he continues to follow them. Then, he acts in accordance with what he sees.

Often counselees will *say* that they will do something or other, and they may even have very good intentions to do it, but when the going gets tough they may give up. That may destroy several weeks of successful counseling. But if they know that their counselor will follow through, that *all* homework assignments will *always* be checked, that a full explanation of any failures to do assignments will be expected, and that any help of any legitimate sort always will be available, that knowledge will help them to carry on in spite of the difficulties that may arise.

At the end of his psalm of contrition, after David has dealt with his own sin, out of his own experience he offers counseling help to others. Evidently, his own problems taught him that supervision is of crucial importance. That's why he puts the matter right up front.

Moreover, counselees (*most* of them) get stuck somewhere along the way. Many times they think that they are following directions when, in fact, they have misread or misapplied them. The counselor who supervises can set them straight before they wander too far off the track or develop wrong patterns. Others may be following directions well enough until they meet an unforeseen difficulty about which they have not yet been instructed. Counselors who supervise can step in to give the instruction that is needed.

Furthermore, supervising enables the counselor to encourage the counselee when he is doing well, to point out *why* certain blessings came his way, etc. And, in doing so, he also may help the counselee to sharpen and to refine his responses so that he may perform more skillfully the task in which he is engaged.

I do not think that I must elaborate further on the values and benefits of good[1] supervision (a word that, incidentally, has close etymological connec-

---

1. Poor supervision is picky, the supervisor often jumps in too soon, never lets counselees struggle or fail, etc.

tions with the idea of *having one's eye on another*). Surely, these few brief comments will stir up many other similar thoughts in the mind of every serious lay counselor. However, the other element in counseling follow through—teaching and training—might not be quite so evident.

Teaching and Training

"I thought that you had to teach the counselee everything that he needs to know *before* you set him on a course of action," you may object. Of course you must teach him all that you can about his contemplated assignment beforehand. But there are many things that cannot be taught until one is involved in the action and/or until he has completed his task. To think that teaching in counseling is all theoretical, all skull practice on the blackboard before the game, is a serious error that must be corrected. No football coach, no piano teacher, no swimming instructor would settle for any such nonsense; why then should Christian counselors? Instead you'll hear them saying such things as "Look, Bill, you need to get more of your shoulder into those tackles; now go out there and get 'em," "Sally, you did very well that time, but let me show you how to play that tough series of chords a bit more smoothly," "Class, I noticed that just about all of you had your face out of the water. That won't do; instead, . . ." And, during half time and at the end of the game, again the coach is at it explaining, correcting, teaching, exhorting. The counselor, among other things, must be a coach. He knows that David is right—there must be instruction and training in the way to go (cf. also the fourth factor in II Tim. 3:16). Coaching involves instruction and encouragment throughout the period of follow through.

This training and teaching consists of correction, practice and generalizing.

Correction and refinement of practice is an element of teaching that is too obvious to spell out in detail. I have already mentioned it here and there under supervision.

Practice in developing new life patterns (cf. Heb. 5; II Tim. 3) is also essential and has been discussed in chapter 3.

Generalizing is, perhaps, a new thought to some. Let me try to explain it to you. Until one has learned not only how to apply a biblical principle to the specific counseling problem to which it is directed but also how to generalize, or apply it to other specific problems as well, the chances are that he has not yet learned how to use the biblical principle.

Take, for instance, a case in which a woman used the principle of

II Corinthians 4 that encourages us to follow responsibilities rather than feelings, to deal with depression that arose over duties that she had neglected. Having successfully mastered this application, at a later time she was able to use the principle in an entirely unexpected circumstance. Her unsaved brother was dying in the hospital. She asked herself, "What is my responsibility toward him?" (not "How do I feel"). She knew immediately that she must witness to him, whether she felt like it or not. She did witness to him and he professed faith in Christ. Because during counseling follow through she had learned to generalize the principle to a number of situations, when her brother became ill months later, she could continue to use the principle. Follow through led to continuation of use.

So, in order to be sure that problems (1) are solved, (2) are solved well, and (3) will continue to be solved, the counselor must take the time to commit himself (and to encourage the counselee to commit himself) to a period of follow through. Again, to do something properly requires the commitment of both the counselor and the counselee. Explain to the counselee *why* it is necessary to spend another two or three weeks even after he has gotten relief and wants to quit: "I could let you go now, but you probably would be back here again in a few months. It is important to learn how to avoid problems in the future and how to handle those that you can't avoid. I want to make sure that you know how to use the biblical principles that we've been working with to meet the new situations you're going to encounter."

Chapter Fourteen

USING HOMEWORK

From time to time I have mentioned the use of homework. Frankly, I don't care what you call it, but just be sure you *don't* call it homework when counseling kids in school! For them you can call it "working on projects" or something of the sort. What I am talking about when I refer to homework is the work that grows out of faith.

Whenever a counselee comes to believe that some teaching of the Scriptures applies to his life in a particular way he is obligated to implement that teaching so that it becomes operative in daily living and, especially, in the reaching of the solution to his problem(s). More than that, if he loves Jesus Christ, he will *want* to do so to please Him—even if his feelings are all to the contrary. Faith leads to works. Homework is a part of the work to which faith leads.

When a problem has been analyzed biblically and biblical solutions to it have been found; it is necessary to implement those solutions. Otherwise, the whole effort amounts to nothing more than an unproductive intellectual exercise. Such intellectualizing does not bring about change for the good. Homework can make the difference. Biblical counselors have found homework to be one of the most vital and effective forces that they can marshall in counseling. But every homework assignment must be accepted and done as a commitment to God, calling upon and relying upon the Holy Spirit to enable the counselee to fulfil it God's way for God's honor.

In summary fashion, let me make a few important suggestions regarding homework:

1. *Use homework every week*. Begin assigning homework at the very first session. There is always something, no matter how small, that the counselee can do about his problem at any point in time. Find it; assign it. No one who met Jesus ever had to go away from Him the same person; he could change *some* way that very day. The biblical counselor, who introduces counselees

72

to Christ in His Word, may (indeed, *must*) look for the same thing in every session.

In the first or second sessions, a counselee may be given assignments designed

(1) to uncover more data ("check out your finances and bring in last month's budget"; "keep a record of every situation in which you find it hard to control your temper");

(2) to lead to repentance, confession, or commitments required to move ahead ("ask God's forgiveness when you genuinely mean it, then see Barbara and ask her forgiveness too");

(3) to help him to examine his life ("make a list of all of the ways in which you are failing God and others as a person, as a husband, as a father and as an employee").

2. *Set patterns of expectation of change from the outset.* Homework assignments are a clear sign that you have such expectations. Of course, you can't do everything right away or all at once. You must set priorities according to knowledge, present ability, sequential factors ("that can't be done until this is first accomplished") and so forth. When something is fulfilled to get started—even one or two small, simple assignments—hope begins to grow for all concerned. Small changes in behavior can lead to large changes in the attitude of both the counselee and others who are involved. If a pattern of change is not set from the first session on,

(1) it will be hard to sustain counseling ("Why go back there? Nothing ever happens; all we do is talk!");

(2) hope soon will diminish ("I don't think we're getting anywhere");

(3) later on you will have to break down earlier patterns that you yourself set ("What do you mean 'homework,' I thought all we were supposed to do was to talk about it?"). That is very foolish.

3. *Homework helps you to evaluate counselees.* The account of the rich young ruler (Matt. 19:16ff.) is an excellent case in point. When given a homework assignment, "Go, sell all that you have . . . ," he went away sadly. He wanted no part of that sort of counsel. So long as he could intellectualize over points of theology in the law, he'd stay and listen. When Christ's theology bit and pinched, he got out fast. He didn't mean business. He wasn't good, as he thought he was, because his response to the homework assignment revealed that he loved riches more than Christ. Similarly, you will find out quickly who means business and who does not. You will not waste time when you use homework. Also, homework may bring conviction of sin.

It is always wrong to hang on the phone week after week while Mary pours out the same old recital of problems, etc. Not only is it sin to allow her to gossip about her husband that way, but it is counterproductive. Tell her what to *do* about her problems, what God requires, and you will soon get fewer calls because (1) she will have done them and her problems will be growing fewer in number or (2) she will find someone else to call who will only listen rather than offer biblical solutions. Either way, you'll gain a couple additional hours a week!

4. *Written homework keeps expectations clear.* Counselees are often highly emotional when they are in the counseling session. As a result, they may miss points you make, forget others and misinterpret and distort much. Write out all homework *in detail*. If there is any doubt about how a counselee will understand your words, spell the assignment out, often underlining points, writing out the opposite ("What I *don't* mean is . . ."), putting things in order (Do this *first"*), etc. Written homework helps keep down arguments between counselees ("He said . . . ," "No he didn't; I distinctly heard him say . . ."). The last thing you want to do is to give counselees an occasion for further argument with each other. Nor can counselees argue with you when you spelled it all out (clearly) in their homework books ("There it is in black and white"). At the end of the session, before the closing prayer, it is always good to read over the homework assignments

    (1) to make sure they are clear to all concerned;
    (2) to make sure there is a basic commitment to them.

These assignments then often become the focus of the closing prayer and the counselee leaves with them in his mind and in his hand.

5. *A written homework book[1] is a constant reminder.* The physical presence of the book in the counselee's possession often acts as counselor in the home, encouraging and reminding the counselee of his obligations for the week. More than once counselees have told me how it prodded them on in their efforts, reminding them of their commitments to Christ.

6. *Homework speeds up counseling.* The changes that God requires of counselees are not confined to the counseling sessions when they are designated for the period between sessions in homework. Of course, some

---

1. Homework books are available through C.S.S., 1790 E. Willow Grove Ave., Laverock, PA, 19118.

changes—especially in thought and attitude, and in commitments made—are made in counseling sessions. But the large changes in relationships, growth in adopting new patterns, etc., that also are so crucial to counseling, occur all week long in actual life situations. Moreover, in so simple a matter as data gathering, in one week a counselee can gather and put into condensed form as many data as you might be able to extract only after five or six sessions of probing for it. Why waste everyone's time?

7. *Homework eliminates counselor dependency.* When the counseling focus is on how the counselee will live before God and his neighbor during the coming week rather than on what the "expert" can do during the magic hour, that

    (1) changes the locus of responsibility for change from the counselor to the counselee, and
    (2) teaches the counselee to depend on God rather than on the counselor.

8. *Homework is a yardstick.* It is easy for both counselors and counselees to deceive themselves about the progress that has (or has not) been made in counseling. Rereading previous assignments can give a pretty good idea about how far counseling has progressed at any given point. In this way, encouragment, hope, warning, rebuke, etc., can be applied to the situation on the basis of factual evidence ("What do you mean when you say 'I haven't done anything?' Look at these 15 assignments that you have fulfilled. Now, of course, if there is something you haven't told me about, that you ought to be doing, I certainly would like to know about that").

9. *Homework provides a personalized guide for reference.* Counselees can reread a homework book regularly in order to prevent future failure, may turn to it at critical moments of temptation for help and will use it from time to time to extricate themselves from problems into which they may have fallen.

All in all, then, you can see that homework is a very important element in counseling. Each counselor must learn how to adapt biblical principles in practical, concrete and creative ways to the peculiarities of each counselee's situation. After a while he will develop a stockpile of basic assignments that, by making variations of these themes, he will find useful again and again.

But, regularly, he also will encounter circumstances that demand fresh, on-the-spot assignments that he never used before. A good place to discover a great number of worthwhile assignments is in Wayne Mack's *A Homework Manual for Biblical Counselors*, vols. I, II.[2]

---

2. Available through C.S.S., 1790 E. Willow Grove Ave., Laverock, PA, 19118.

Chapter Fifteen

PROBLEMS FREQUENTLY FACED

In this book it is neither necessary nor useful to take up a great number of problems; this is an elementary textbook. Therefore, I have decided to discuss only six of the seven areas that I think Christian laymen are likely to encounter most often. They are:

1. Marriage problems
2. Family problems
3. Guidance problems
4. Depression problems
5. Anger problems
6. Forgiveness problems
7. Discipline problems

Since I have already spent some time dealing with discipline in a previous chapter I shall omit any discussion here. And, because of the closeness of the subjects, I shall combine my discussion of items 1 and 2.

Again, rather than attempt to treat each topic at length, I shall consider each concisely, getting to some of the most essential principles and practices pertinent to each. But, remember, what I do here is more suggestive than exhaustive. Keep this in mind. For more detail and fuller treatments, see my other books.

Marriage and Family

I shall simply run through some of the major principles that a counselor must know in order to deal with marriage and family problems. I cannot establish these biblically here, though I have done so elsewhere. Occasionally, I shall note a key biblical reference.

Marriage problems stem from (1) wrong understandings of marriage, (2) selfish attitudes and practices, and (3) failure to know how (and unwillingness) to make, implement and to keep biblical commitments to God and to one's marriage partner.

Christian counselors must understand and be ready to affirm the truths that

1. Marriage is not of human origin but was ordained by God who
2. Instituted it as the first and most basic building block of all human societies, including political government and the church.
3. It was ordained not to provide for legalized sexual activity, or to propagate the human race (marriage is more than mating) but, rather,
4. Was instituted to solve the problem of loneliness (Gen. 2:18). It is also
5. A covenantal arrangement (Prov. 2:17; Mal. 2:14) that is brought about by contract (not by fornication) and
6. May properly be referred to as *The Covenant of Companionship* (Prov. 2:17; Mal. 2:14) in which
7. Two persons promise to provide for one another companionship of the most intimate sort (Gen. 2:25; 2:18), including a sexual relationship in which
8. Each determines to satisfy the other's needs rather than to seek his own pleasure (I Cor. 7:3-5), and by which
9. They will raise holy children for the Lord (Gen. 1:28; I Cor. 7:14).
10. Children and work must never take priority over one's marriage partner.
11. The marriage relationship is permanent (Matt. 19:6) while the parent-child relationship is temporary (Gen. 2:24) and must be broken as
12. A man leaves father and mother and cleaves so closely to his wife that
13. They can be called "one flesh" (i.e., one *person;* Eph. 5:22-33; Gen. 2:24).
14. When a man fails to make a clean break with his parents, the emerging marriage suffers and the wife is pitted against her in-laws.
15. A husband is to assume the obligations of loving leadership as the head of his home (Eph. 5:22-33),
16. Using all the help that his wife brings to decision-making as well as in other ways (Gen. 2:18), and
17. She is to submit to him (Eph. 5:22-24; I Pet. 3:1) in all matters over which God has given him authority in the home,
18. That submission consisting of respect and obedience (Eph. 5, I Pet. 3).
19. The marriage covenant is broken only by death and divorce, and
20. A sinful divorce (all divorces are occasioned by sin, but not all are sinful; cf. Jer. 3:8) breaks a marriage, even though it ought not to have been issued (Deut. 24:1-4; I Cor. 7:10,11).

21. Separation is unbiblical (I Cor. 7:5), and divorce among believers is legitimate only in cases of sexual sin (Matt. 5; 19) while

22. The divorce of a believer from an unbeliever may be legitimate when the unbeliever wants to break up the marriage (I Cor. 7:15). Otherwise, the believer must continue the marriage (I Cor. 7:15).

23. In all other cases, by reconciliation and church discipline (Matt. 18: 15ff.), it is possible to resolve differences between believers.

24. Children must be raised by the sort of discipline and counsel that God uses in raising His children (Eph. 6:4) and

25. The rod (corporal punishment) and reproof (spiritual counsel) will be used (Prov. 29:15).

These 25 principles, along with many others, have been spelled out in more detail in my other books (esp. *Competent to Counsel, The Christian Counselor's Manual, Christian Living in the Home* and *Marriage, Divorce and Remarriage*), where an exposition of the biblical references is also given. For help in doing premarital counseling, see Howard Eyrich's book, *Three to Get Ready*.

Guidance

Much misinformation, confused and confusing advice and just plain error is abroad about guidance. For instance, the two biblical references to being "led by the Spirit" have nothing whatever to do with guidance and decision-making. They both refer to sanctification, the process of walking in righteousness.

All guidance comes from the Scriptures. Today, God no longer speaks in visions or dreams as He did when producing the Bible (Heb. 2:1ff.), or by other means of direct revelation like the prophets and apostles had (Eph. 3:5; 4:11; II Cor. 12:12—These were *foundational* gifts to the church, now removed since the foundation was laid). Moreover, so-called promptings, checks in the spirit, hunches, etc., must be rejected as means of discerning God's will. It is wrong to look to circumstances, put out the fleece, search for open and closed doors. The Holy Spirit did not take hundreds of years to produce the Bible only to by-pass it. No, in the Bible are all things necessary for life and godliness. From the Bible alone, every decision may be made; it is sufficient.

When counselors allow counselees to look anywhere else for guidance, they will encourage them to go wrong. In the end, all of these other methods turn out to be nothing more than (1) following one's own subjective wishes, feelings and desires (which so often are untrustworthy), or (2) a matter of being led by the will of another human being.

God's will is found in the Bible. But it appears in two forms: directly applicable Scripture; indirectly applicable Scripture. Sometimes biblical commands and principles apply directly to the problems at hand as when one is tempted to pilfer and remembers the commandment "You must not steal" or when he reads "Don't let the sun set on your anger." Such applications are easy to make, if not always easy to follow. It is when one must apply principles indirectly (and usually more than one) to box in legitimate alternatives that difficulty appears. Questions like "Shall I take this job or that one?" are not so readily answered. And it is here that people start looking for easy ways out.

To questions like that, several principles usually must be applied. In the example of the job choice, just mentioned, here are a couple of the biblical principles that would be brought to bear on a decision:
1. Is the job biblically legitimate (robbery, prostitution, etc., are not)?
2. In which of the several legitimate job opportunities that remain do I have the opportunity to fully use my God-given gifts?
3. Which job will enable me to provide for my family adequately?

These, along with any other pertinent principles not mentioned, will be used to exclude a number of jobs. Thus the range of choices will be narrowed. If only one job remains, the decision has been made.

But, suppose, after applying all of the relevant biblical principles to the situation, there are still four jobs remaining, all of which are legitimate possibilities; what does one do then? *He is free to choose on the basis of expedience and preference.*

There are many who (wrongly) suppose that God will in some definitive way make even this final choice for them. It is this false idea that leads to seeking guidance in gimmicks and that brings so much agony and grief. Actually instead, one should enjoy the freedom that he has been granted. There is no need to agonize over doors and fleece.

The Bible teaches that we worship the God of abundance; He is the God of leftovers! It wouldn't have been wrong to take *any* piece of bread when Christ multiplied the loaves, but *one had to choose*—there was such abundance that there were twelve baskets full left over.

When, therefore, the choice is between things not different enough in principle to make a difference, the final decision among them is left to us. We are freed from the agony of having to narrow every selection to "the *only* right one." *Every* piece of bread was right; there was no *one* piece that was *the* and the *only* right one to take. That means that we don't have to make moral choices between which pair of socks or which ties we wear so long as all of those clothes that we choose among fit the general biblical principles of modesty and moderation.

In working with counselees, you must emphasize these two facts:
1. All applicable biblical principles must be brought to bear on the decision to narrow the possibilities;
2. If options yet remain, one may decide on a preferential/expediential basis.

Of course, both of these steps must be taken prayerfully, since God works in general providence to help us, even when He does not give us direct revelation.

To these two principles must be added a third: the *Holding Principle:* one must not move ahead until he is sure that the action he is about to take is not sin (Rom. 14:23).

The greatest problem that you will have with counselees is in teaching them how to prayerfully use their heads in a biblical manner in decision-making. The many false methods of "discovering God's will" through flip-and-point procedures, spreading the fleece, or whatever, all have one thing in common—the counselee doesn't have to think and he can hold God responsible for the decision. The biblical method requires work: Bible study coupled with thinking. The counselee himself makes a responsible decision with God's help.

Depression

While there is a small possibility that some problems of depression may stem from chemical causes, there is little reason to believe they do. Experience in helping depressed persons has shown that most, if not all, cases of depression arise from failure to assume or to carry out one's God-given responsibilities.

There is no space to develop the passage adequately, but in II Corinthians 4 Paul makes it very clear that even the enormous pressures that were exerted on him were not able to depress him. Contrary to the thinking of many today who think that pressure leads to depression, Paul asserts,

> Since we have this service to perform as the result of mercy, *we don't give up* (II Cor. 4:1),

and then went on to say,

81

We are afflicted in all sorts of ways, *but not crushed;* perplexed but *not given to despair* (II Cor. 4:8),

and, finally,

As a result, *we don't give up* (II Cor. 4:16).

The depressed person has "given up;" if any phrase describes him it is that. He is "crushed," and "given to despair." But Paul did not give up. What kept him from doing so even under pressures like those described in II Corinthians 11:23ff. and II Corinthians 6:4-10? He tells us in verse 1: he had a God-given service to perform that, out of love and gratitude for God's mercy, he would perform—no matter what!

Popularly, the word *depression* is used to mean a "blue" or "down" period. Technically, however, the word refers to one who sees no use of going on, and is in such great despair that he (usually it is *she*[1]) gives up and ceases to function in life's normal activities. She gives up on her normal responsibilities and lies around in despair saying "I can't." She isn't down; she is down-and-out.

What you must understand as a counselor is that a depressed person thinks she *can't* do something because she is in despair when, actually, she is in despair *because* she fails to fulfil her God-given obligations. Depression occurs when one continues to handle a down period wrongly. Down periods come to all (as the aftermath of sickness, because of guilt, etc.). But Paul handled them rightly; that's why when afflicted, he wasn't crushed, when perplexed, he did not give in to despair. He was often down, but never down-and-out (depressed).

When a down period is wrongly handled, the counselee spirals downward into depression. The key factor is *how* one handles a down period; that is what makes all the difference. If a woman follows her feelings when down, she will "put off" her responsibilities (until she "feels like doing them"). But she will be in trouble: *persons who give in to their feelings give up on their responsibilities.* Then, out of guilt and out of frustration as things pile up, they feel worse, give into *those* feelings, shirk more responsibilities, feel worse, and so on and on till they reach the bottom of the hole.

In order to help a depressed person, therefore, the counselor must get her once again to assume her responsibilities ("go do the shopping and make all the meals this week") REGARDLESS OF HOW SHE FEELS. She will

---

1. Statistics show that twice as many get depressed as men.

82

protest: "I can't." But the counselor must insist "If you are physically able, you *can*, and you *must, whether you feel like it or not.* You don't have to *feel* like shopping and cooking; you just have to *do* it." When she does so, she will begin to feel better and she will spiral upward.

The way to prevent depression from occurring in the future, similarly, is to train her to assume her responsibilities, especially in a down period, even (especially) when she doesn't feel like doing so. Paul followed this practice (v. 1) and that is why, under trials and afflictions greater than any your counselees will bear, he never became depressed. Make it clear throughout that this a matter of faith and love toward Christ.

Anger

In and of itself, anger is not wrong. God gets angry daily (Ps. 7:11), Jesus was angry (Mark. 3:5) and believers may be angry too (Eph. 4:26). Two things make anger sinful:

1. When it is occasioned for biblically improper reasons (e.g., pride, hurt feelings);
2. When righteous anger is expressed in the wrong way.

Two sinful expressions of righteously occasioned anger are blowing up (Prov. 29:11; Eph. 4:31) and clamming up (Eph. 4:26). Anger is designed to destroy something. In both of these sinful expressions of anger it destroys persons (others, one's self). Only God and the state, to which He has given such authority, have the right to destroy persons.

The angry counselee, therefore, must be taught to *express* his anger (not clam up) *under control* (not blow up), by directing its destructive force toward problems that have arisen, to destroy (or solve) them (Eph. 4:29b), rather than toward persons (Eph. 4:29a).

Counselees will tell you that they *can't* control anger; and yet they do—where they have *learned* to do so (at work, at school, etc.). They express uncontrolled anger also, only where they have learned to do so (usually at home). Pointing this out may help you to get under way.

Forgiveness

Sometimes the basic counseling problem is lack of forgiveness; more often, it plays a complicating role. Counselees must be ready to forgive whenever another says that he repents (Luke. 17:3ff.). They forgive, not because of the other person alone, but principally out of gratitude and love for Christ (Eph. 4:32).

Seeking forgiveness is not apologizing. Apologizing ("I'm sorry") is simply an expression of one's feelings. In an apology, one confesses no wrong and asks for nothing from the other; the ball is still in his own hands at the end of an apology. That means that the matter has not really been brought to a conclusion. On the contrary, one who seeks forgiveness says, "I wronged you; will you forgive me?" He confesses sin and tosses the ball to the other fellow, who is now obligated by the Bible to say "yes" and thus close the matter forever.

Forgiveness is *granted* to another only when he seeks it, but internally one forgives (i.e., he no longer holds on to the offense as something that could turn to bitterness) in his heart in prayer (Mark. 11:25). Forgiveness is a promise. When God forgives, He says, "I will remember your sins against you no more." A promise can be made and kept whether one *feels* like doing so or not. When one grants forgiveness to another he promises:

1. not to raise the matter to him again;
2. not to tell others about it;
3. not to think about it himself.

Often counselees will ask, "Must I forgive *and* forget?" The answer to this is that one must forgive *in order to* forget. Only by making and keeping the threefold promise can one forget. But when he promises, and keeps the promise, he will forget much faster than he thinks he can. When a person claims that he has forgiven another but "just can't forget," he isn't keeping his promise and must himself seek forgiveness for breaking it.

Another question sometimes arises: "What do I do now—Mary won't forgive me?" If Mary is a Christian, follow Matthew 18:15ff.; if she is not, follow Romans 12:18.

These glimpses of problems common to counseling must suffice. Though they are brief, they do contain the pith of what one needs to know and may serve as reminders of what to do. Often one or more of these problems is intertwined with others (e.g., marriage problems may occasion—not *cause* —depression and may involve forgiveness). To handle complex situations like this, separate each problem out of the whole (as Paul does in I Corinthians) and deal individually with it in order of priority (e.g., "we can't deal with the question of poor sexual relations until there is mutual forgiveness and commitment to solving problems God's way).

It is my hope that this chapter may become a resource to which you refer regularly.

Chapter Sixteen

HOW TO GROW AS A COUNSELOR

Doubtless, even from studying this book, you have discovered that an effective biblical counselor is one who knows much about God's Word, knows much about how to put it into practice in concrete life situations and is, himself, a growing Christian. How does one grow as a counselor?

First, he grows as a Christian. I shall not elaborate on this, since there is much already available on the subject (not all good; not all bad either). My concern is to focus on helps available that can enhance his growth *as a counselor*. We shall assume that he is growing already as a Christian (I know that the two are not so readily separable, but I make the distinction simply for the sake of convenience).

Secondly, he must grow as a biblical student and practitioner. He must learn how to study and use the Bible effectively since he will be giving not his own counsel, but God's. Effective Bible usage involves:

1. A willingness to follow the Bible wherever it leads, even when it smashes your prejudices and cherished ideas;
2. Ability to interpret Scripture by Scripture;
3. Concern to find out the historical-grammatical meaning of each passage in order to
4. Discover the *telos* (purpose) in each passage (i.e., What did the Holy Spirit intend to do to a person through this portion of Scripture?);
5. Having found the *telos*, an uncompromising dedication to the principle that he will use the passage for no other purposes than that (or those) for which the Holy Spirit gave it;
6. A willingness to spend long, hard (but joyous) hours studying the Scriptures, using commentaries, and other helps designed to assist one on coming to an understanding of difficult passages and knotty problems;
7. Ability to use the Scriptures practically by concretely applying and implementing biblical principles first in one's own life, and then in the lives of those he counsels.

Thirdly, he must grow as a student of biblical counseling practice. Ten years ago, materials to help him were not available. Now, I shall be able to list quite a few, all of which are available through Christian Study Services, 1790 E. Willow Grove Ave., Laverock, PA., 19118. Here they are:

MY BOOKS

Competent to Counsel. This work calls the Christian counselor back to the Bible as the only foundation on which to construct a counseling model.

The Christian Counselor's Manual. A 475-page, in-depth study of counseling problems and their biblical solutions. The one counseling book to buy if you can buy only one.

The Christian Counselor's New Testament. An *original* translation of the New Testament. It includes these counseling helps: • Marginal notes on counseling principles • Shaded passages of help to counselors • Index of biblical references helpful in dealing with specific problems.

The Christian Counselor's Casebook. True case descriptions with probing questions to prompt discussion and learning of key counseling principles.

Christian Living in the Home. The biblical themes of marriage, communication, sex, children are presented.

Coping with Counseling Crises. Step by step analysis of what's needed when you have to help someone through a crisis.

Four Weeks with God and Your Neighbor. A devotional workbook for counselees and others. Designed for use with counselees as part of homework assignments. Aids in pinpointing sinful patterns and provides a means to leading a more consistent Christian life.

How to Overcome Evil. A series of lectures that show how to deal with unbelievers. For counselors and counselees.

The Big Umbrella. Collected essays on various counseling topics including, "Is Society Sick?," "Grief as a Counseling Opportunity," "Drugs and Your Child" and many more.

The Use of the Scriptures in Counseling. The place, significance and application of the Bible to today's counseling problems.

Lectures in Counseling. This volume brings together three previous titles: *Your Place in the Counseling Revolution, The Use of Scriptures in Counseling* and *Coping with Counseling Crisis.* New lectures are: *The Student-Pastor Counselor Today* and *Counseling and the Sovereignty of God.*

Trust and Obey. A Practical Commentary on I Peter. This book provides a full commentary on the book of I Peter, stressing the overall theme of the book, "How to Handle Suffering." The commentary is for serious Bible students, with a view to showing the relevance of each passage to preaching and counseling.

The Power of Error, demonstrated in an actual counseling case. This complete analysis of a case contrasts the methodology and effects of nouthetic with other counseling procedures.

Matters of Concern to Christian Counselors. A Potpourri of Principles and Practices.

More than Redemption. A thorough investigation and presentation of the theological foundations of nouthetic counseling. This work studies the doctrine of man (and lays the substructure of the long-awaited counseling anthropology), redemption, prayer as well as the whole field of systematic theology . . . all with a view to practical, counseling application. If you want to know how Christian theology informs your counseling model, then don't miss this work. "The most significant work from the pen of Dr. Adams since *Competent to Counsel.*"—John Bettler.

Update on Christian Counseling. Vol. I. Surveys biblical teaching on current counseling concerns, e.g., Failure in Counseling, Drugs and Counseling, Getting Organized, etc.

Update on Christian Counseling. Vol. II.

What about Nouthetic Counseling? Questions asked to learn from and *attack* nouthetic counseling are answered in a straight-forward manner.

Your Place in the Counseling Revolution. Defense of the pastor as God's primary counselor for troubled people.

Booklets: *Christ and Your Problems; Godliness through Discipline; What to Do about Worry.* Great as handouts!

Pamphlets: Fear . . . Depression . . . Worry . . . Marriage . . . Anger . . . Hooked

Prayers for Troubled Times. Prayers written in simple, everyday English reverently express the heartfelt and inner cries of God's people. A counseling aid.

Marriage, Divorce and Remarriage. Deals with all three areas biblically.

The Christian Counselor's Handbook

Other Counseling Aids . . .

The Journal of Pastoral Practice. Vol. I, No. 1; Vol. I, No. 2; Vol. II, No. 1; Vol. II, No. 2; Vol. III, No. 1; Vol. III, No. 2; Vol. III, No. 3

Christian Counselor's Starter Packet. Hundreds of personal data forms, counseling record sheets, homework assignments and other aids to a counseling ministry.

OTHER BOOKS BY NOUTHETIC COUNSELORS

By Dr. Wayne Mack:

A Homework Manual for Biblical Counselors. If you do any counseling at all, you cannot afford to be without this book. It contains practical, down-to-earth assignments which are thoroughly biblical and get people moving toward solutions to their problems. Assignments on anger, anxiety, communication, loneliness and many other topics. Over two hundred pages.

How to Develop Deep Unity in the Marriage Relationship. A manual to be used by husband and wife together. Step-by-step lessons, with appropriate exercises, take a couple through all the important scriptural aspects of marriage. Extremely helpful . . . very practical.

How to Pray Effectively and *How to Read the Bible.* These study guides with the "How To" of the two most vital exercises of the Christian life. Practical and solidly biblical.

Dr. Mack is on the counseling staff at Christian Counseling & Educational Foundation and has an extensive seminar and lecture ministry.

By Dr. Robert Somerville:

Help for Hotliners. A pastor of the Evangelical Free Church, Dr. Somerville explains how to use the phone effectively when you receive that emergency call.

By Dr. Howard Eyrich:

Three to Get Ready. A manual on premarital counseling presenting a step-by-step guide through the major areas to be covered. Chock full of practical advice. The premarital counseling guide you have been waiting for.

What to Do When (editor). Collection of addresses presented at the second annual meeting of the National Association of Nouthetic Counselors.

Dr. Eyrich is the Southeastern representative of CCEF and maintains a counseling and teaching ministry in both Atlanta and Macon, Georgia.

By Dr. Richard Ganz (editor):

Thou Shalt Not Kill. The Christian Case against Abortion. Abortion concerns every Christian. Here you will find evidence written by medical, psychological, legal and sociological experts which conclude that abortion on demand is anti-Christian. Written with the layman and professional in mind.

By George Scipione:

Timothy, Titus and You. A study guide of the pastoral Epistles for pastors, elders and deacons. How should the church be led? This solidly biblical book written by a pastor and board member of CCEF will give you exciting and probing answers.

CASSETTE TAPES

By Dr. Jay E. Adams:

Competent to Counsel Training Series. For persons who cannot attend CCEF training sessions. Also excellent for small group study involving church officers and key laymen. Designed for training Christians in the basic techniques of biblical counseling.

JABC-1	Should a Christian Be Able to Counsel? Instilling Hope in the Counselee.
JABC-2	God's Standard and Program for Change, God's Methodology for Change.
JABC-3	Question-Asking Techniques, The Need for Homework in Counseling.
JABC-4	Questions and Answers: What is marriage? Dr. Adams, how did you develop your techniques? How do biblical principles of counseling apply to counseling non-Christians? Marriage & Family Problems.
JABC-5	Handling Anger God's Ways, Dealing with Depression.
JABC-6	Managing the Time God Gives Us—Schizophrenia. Role Play Cases and Critiques I.
JABC-7	Role Play Cases and Critiques II.
JABC-8	Questions and Answers: How do you counsel deep depression? How do you counsel people who overwork? Should a wife ever step in as a spiritual leader? Questions and Answers in Setting Up a Training Program.

Crisis Counseling Series. Designed to train Christian counselors to handle situations where immediate action is necessary.

JA 201   Crisis Counseling—AID
JA 202   Crisis Counseling—Analysis
JA 203   Crisis Counseling—Inventory
JA 204   Crisis Counseling—Direction
JA 205   Questions and Answers: Are certain gifts specially suited for counseling? What if a person has a problem and is not aware of it?
JA 206   Listening in Counseling
JA 207   The Use of Talk in Counseling
JA 208   Dr. Richard Ganz, "How I Became a Christian Counselor." Dr. Adams, Questions and Answers: Is masturbation for Christians?
JA 209   Questions and Answers: How would you counsel a woman whose husband is physically abusive to his wife and children? How does interchurch discipline work?
JA 210   *Role Play Cases and Critiques I: Wife's Husband is Leaving; A Potential Suicide
JA 211   *Role Play Cases and Critiques II: Wife Won't Speak; Homosexuality; Wife with Cancer
JA 212   *Role Play Cases and Critiques III: Wife's Husband Dies; Mother's Baby Born Deformed; Pregnant Unwed Daughter
JA 213   *Role Play Cases and Critiques IV: Husband Wants Wife-Swapping; Wife is Leaving Husband

*All role plays in this series *do not* appear in the Competent to Counsel Training Series.

The Sovereignty of God in Counseling.
JA 301   Sovereignty of God in Counseling

Radio Talk Tapes. The following cassettes are taken from Dr. Adams' Radio Program. There is no duplication of material from the previous four sets of cassettes.

JA 401   Marriage Is Made in Heaven; The Purpose of Marriage; Singled Out by God; Companionship in Intimacy; Leaving and Cleaving.
JA 402   Headship: Wife's Joy; You Are Your Husband's Helper; The

	Husband Is the Head of His Wife; The Husband as Loving Leader; The Husband as a Student of His Wife
JA 403	Children: Solve Problems God's Way; Getting on Teaching Terms; Show and Tell; Regular Discipline; Returning Good for Evil; Proper Motives; Facing Up to Your Problems; No Blame Shifting; Do Things Right Away
JA 404	Winning Your Unsaved Husband
JA 405	Proper Submission to the Proper Authorities; The Devil Made Me Do It; Doing Work That Pleases God; Is Masturbation for Christians? Why Did *This* Happen to *Me?*; How to Handle a Potential Suicide.
JA 406	Effective Communication; Ministering to Disabled People; Inferiority Complex; Winning Your Unsaved Wife; Be Prepared for Counseling
JA 407	Christian Forgiveness; Christian Responsibility, or Blame Shifting?
JA 408	The Fear of Death; Church Discipline; Being in the Hospital
JA 409	Accepting Retarded Children; How to Handle Trouble; Forgiving an Adulterous Mate; The Conscience
JA 410	Am I Too Old to Change? Talking About Problems?; Drunkenness; The Christian Answer; Breaking Old Habits; Transactional Analysis for Christians?; Learn to Love.

Biblical Forgiveness. 8 tapes survey what the Bible says about: Man's Need for Forgiveness ● The Meaning and Basis of God's Forgiveness ●Jesus' Command to Forgive ● Forgiveness: Promise or Feeling ● Judging Your Brother ● Church Discipline ● Seeking Forgiveness ● Confession

Father and Husband in the Home. This series was given at Reformed Laymen's Fellowship seminars at Westminster Theological Seminary in 1975.

| JA RO1 | The Role of the Husband and Father in the Home—Part I |
| JA RO2 | The Role of the Husband and Father in the Home—Part II |

Marriage, Divorce and Remarriage. Eight cassette tapes. You will not find better material on the biblical teaching on divorce and remarriage. All presented with a view to counseling people caught in this growing problem.

By Dr. John Bettler

Counseling Fundamentals. Two cassette tapes present an introduction to the dynamics of biblical counseling. Deals with how to establish involvement, question asking, gathering data, etc. Excellent for individual study or small group presentation to introduce the importance of biblical counseling.

Sane Thoughts about Self. A five-cassette tape series on counseling and the problem of self-image. Originally delivered at the Summer Institute of Pastoral Studies, these lectures present a biblical perspective on the problem of self-image and offer an alternative to both popular psychological and pastoral approaches.

The Friendly Arena: The Christian Home. Six-cassette tapes: A survey of the biblical teaching on marriage. Emphasizes how to handle marital conflict. Includes these titles: "How to Fight with Your Spouse," "Sexes—Opposite or Different?," "How to Forgive Your Spouse," "Communication Workshops," and others.

By Dr. Howard Eyrich
Premarital Counseling

By Dr. Wayne Mack

Developing Deeper Unity in Marriage

WMM1	God's Blueprint for Marriage
WMM2	How to Be a Fulfilled and Fulfilling Wife
WMM3	How to Be a Fulfilled and Fulfilling Husband
WMM4	Handling Family Finances
WMM5	God's Plan for Rearing Children, Part 1—Family Leadership
WMM6	God's Plan for Rearing Children, Part 2—What to Avoid
WMM7	Sex as God Intended
WMM8	Conflict Resolution in Marriage
WMM9	Communication I
WMM10	Communication II
WMM11	Communication III
WMM12	Communication IV
WMM13	Developing Effective Communication
WMM14	God's Plan for Rearing Children, Part 3—Bring Them Up

A Study Guide to be used in conjunction with these tapes on marital unity is available.

Biblical Solutions to Life's Problems

WMBS 1   There Is Help and Hope
WMBS 2   Constructive Anger
WMBS 3   Overcoming Anxiety
WMBS 4   Overcoming Depression
WMBS 5   Getting Along with People: Healing Broken Relationships
WMBS 6   How to Handle Loneliness
WMBS 7   Overcoming Impatience
WMBS 8   Developing an Attitude of Gratitude
WMBS 9   Overcoming Discontentment
WMBS 10   How to Handle the Problem of Old Age
WMBS 11   Biblical Approach to Problem Solving I
WMBS 12   Biblical Approach to Problem Solving II
WMBS 13   Self Pity—The Why Me Syndrome

A Study Guide for the tapes on Biblical Solutions to Life's Problems is available.

There are also available courses of study at training centers around the country. In addition to the Christian Counseling and Educational Center, a list of other centers approved by The National Association of Nouthetic Counselors may be obtained by writing Bob Smith, M.D., 100 Doncaster Dr., Lafayette, Indiana, 47905.

CONCLUSION

In conclusion, let me remind you that studying this book will not make you a biblical counselor. It should help. But it is a *first* book that is designed to acquaint you with biblical counseling, describe your responsibilities as a Christian, help you to get started, and (once begun) help you to improve your performance.

If what you have read whets your appetite, you now know where to turn to find more. If you must seek counseling you know what to look for. If what is done in counseling does not approximate what you have read, find another counselor who counsels biblically. C.C.E.F. maintains a list of biblical counselors. You may call C.C.E.F. at (215) 884-7676.

Most of all, I trust that you will take the command of Galatians 6:1 seriously and you will begin to counsel those whom God providentially places in your way, so that those whose lives are not now useful to Christ's church will be restored to usefulness. If the part that this book plays is to make you in greater measure *ready to restore*, I shall be very grateful to God.

Appendix A

THE PERSONAL DATA INVENTORY

IDENTIFICATION DATA:

Name _____ Phone _____

Address _____

Occupation _____ Bus. Phone _____

Sex _____ Birth Date _____ Age _____

Marital Status: Single_____ Going Steady_____ Married_____

Separated_____ Divorced_____ Widowed_____

Education (last year completed): _____ (grade)

Other training (list type and years) _____

_____

Referred here by _____

Address _____

HEALTH INFORMATION:

Rate your health (check): Very Good____ Good____ Average____

Declining____ Other____

Weight changes recently: Lost_____ Gained_____

List all important present or past illnesses or injuries or handicaps:

_____

_____

Date of last medical examination _____

Report: _____

_____

Your physician _____

Address _____

Are you presently taking medication? Yes____ No____

What _____

Have you ever been arrested? Yes____ No____

State circumstances: _____

_____

Are you willing to sign a release of information form so that your counselor may write for social, psychiatric, or medical report?

Yes____ No____

RELIGIOUS BACKGROUND:

Denominational preference: _____

Member _____

Church attendance per month (circle):   0   1   2   3   4   5   6

7   8   9   10+   Baptized? Yes____ No____

Church attended in childhood _____

Religious background of spouse (if married) _____

Do you consider yourself a religious person? Yes____ No____

Uncertain____

Do you believe in God? Yes____ No____ Uncertain____

Do you pray to God? Never____ Occasionally____ Often____

Are you saved? Yes____ No____ Not sure what you mean _____

How frequently do you read the Bible? Never____ Occasionally_____

Often____ Do you have regular family devotions? Yes____ No _____

Explain recent changes in your religious life, if any _____

_____

MARRIAGE AND FAMILY INFORMATION:

Name of spouse _____

Address _____

Phone _____ Occupation _____

Business phone _____ Your spouse's age _____

Education (in years)____ Religion _____

Is spouse willing to come for counseling? Yes____ No____

Uncertain____ Have you ever been separated? Yes____ No _____

When? from_____ to_____

Has either of you ever filed for divorce? Yes____ No____

When?_____

Date of marriage _____

Your ages when married: Husband_____ Wife _____

How long did you know your spouse before marriage? _____

Length of engagement _____

Give brief information about any previous marriages: _____

_____

Information about children:

PM*	Name	Age	Sex	Living Yes No	Education in years	Marital status

*Check this column if child is by previous marriage

If you were reared by anyone other than your parents, briefly explain:

_____

How many older brothers_____ sisters_____ do you have?

How many younger brothers_____ sisters_____ do you have?

Have there been any deaths in the family during the last year?

Yes_____ No_____ Who and when: _____

_____

PERSONALITY INFORMATION:

Have you used drugs for other than medical purposes?

Yes_____ No_____ What? _____

Have you ever had a severe emotional upset? Yes_____ No_____

Explain _____

_____

Have you ever had any psychotherapy or counseling before?

Yes_____ No_____ If yes, list counselor or therapist and dates:

_____

_____

What was the outcome? _____

Circle any of the following words that best describe you now:

active   ambitious   self-confident   persistent   nervous   hardworking

impatient   impulsive   moody   often-blue   excitable   imaginative

calm   serious   easy-going   shy   good-natured   introvert   extrovert

likable   leader   quiet   hard-boiled   submissive   self-conscious

lonely   sensitive   other _____

Have you ever felt people were watching you? Yes_____ No_____

Do people's faces ever seem distorted? Yes_____ No_____

Do you ever have difficulty distinguishing faces? Yes_____ No_____

Do colors ever seem too bright? _____Too dull? _____

Are you sometimes unable to judge distance? Yes_____ No_____

Have you ever had hallucinations? Yes_____ No_____

Is your hearing exceptionally good? Yes_____ No_____

Do you have problems sleeping? Yes_____ No_____

How many hours of sleep do you average each night? _____

BRIEFLY ANSWER THE FOLLOWING QUESTIONS:

1. What is your problem? (What brings you here?)

2. What have you done about it?

3. What do you want us to do? (What are your expectations in coming here?)

4. What brings you here at this time?

5. Is there any other information we should know?

THE COUNSELOR'S TOPICAL WORKLIST*

On the following pages, alphabetically arranged, there is a list of topics, under each of which appears a limited number of selected Scripture passages. In many ways, this is a curious list, as a quick scanning will indicate. But, to counselors, the peculiar nature of the list is readily understandable and, indeed, constitutes its sole value. It is from beginning to end a counselor's list. It is a worklist, based upon many of the most commonly encountered areas of needs, sins, and problems faced in the counseling context, together with references to key biblical passages that have proven particularly helpful in dealing with each of these topics.

Since the choice of specific Scripture portions will vary from counselor to counselor, according to his understanding and even his interpretation of them, sufficient space has been provided beneath each entry for other references to be added. In this way, by making one's own additions, the list may become a valuable personalized reference source that may be used for many purposes, some of which may extend beyond counseling interests. Plainly, the list is limited, but hopefully it is adequate. Too many topical or scriptural references would confuse the counselor who seeks to obtain quick help (perhaps at times even in the counseling session itself). Indeed, selectivity is what makes the list most useful. Since many persons have asked for just such a list, my expectation is that it will meet a real need.

---

* From Jay E. Adams, *The Christian Counselor's New Testament* (Grand Rapids: Baker Book House), pp. 742-753.

Adultery
Ex. 20:14
II Sam. 11:2
Prov. 2:16-18; 5:1-23;
   6:23-35; 7:5-27; 9:13-16
Hosea, book of
Mal. 2:13-16
Matt. 5:28; 15:19; 19:9
I Cor. 16:9-11

Anxiety (see Worry)

Associations (bad/good)
Prov. 9:6; 13:20; 14:9;
   22:24; 23:20, 21; 29:24
Rom. 16:17, 18
I Cor. 5:9-13
II Cor. 6:14-18
II Tim. 3:5

Alcoholism (see Drunkenness)

Anger
Gen. 4:5-7
Ps. 7:11
Prov. 14:17, 29; 15:1, 18;
   19:11, 19; 20:3, 22; 22:24;
   24:29; 25:15, 28; 29:11, 22
Mark 3:5
Eph. 4:26-32
James 1:19, 20

Assurance
Heb. 4:16; 6:11
I Pet. 1:3-5
II Pet. 1:10
I John 5:13, 18, 19

Avoidance
Gen. 3:8
Prov. 18:1
I Tim. 6:11
II Tim. 2:22

Change
Ezek. 36:25-27
Matt. 16:24
Eph. 4:17-32
Col. 3:1-14
I Thess. 1:9
II Tim. 3:17
Heb. 10:25
James 1:14, 15
I Pet. 3:9

Bitterness (see Resentment)

Blame Shifting
Gen. 3:12, 13
Prov. 19:3

Children (see Family)

Church
Eph. 4:1-16
Heb. 10:25
Rev. 2, 3

Body
Rom. 12:1, 2
I Cor. 3:16, 17; 6:18-20; 15
II Cor. 5:1-4

Commandment
Ex. 20
Prov. 13:13
Luke 17:3-10
John 13:34; 15:12
I John 5:2, 3

Conscience
Mark 6:19
Acts 24:16
Rom. 2:15
I Cor. 8:10, 12
I Tim. 1:5, 19; 3:9
II Tim. 1:3
Heb. 13:18
I Pet. 3:16, 21

Communication
Eph. 4:25-32

Conviction
John 16:7-11
II Tim. 3:17
Jude 15

Confession
Prov. 28:13
James 5:16
I John 1:9

Death
Ps. 23:6
Prov. 3:21-26; 14:32
I Cor. 15:54-58
Phil. 1:21, 23
Heb. 2:14, 15

Decision Making
II Tim. 3:15-17
Heb. 11:23-27

Depression
Gen. 4:6, 7
Ps. 32, 38, 51
Prov. 18:14
II Cor. 4:8, 9

Desire
Gen. 3:6
Ex. 20:17
Prov. 10:3, 24; 11:6; 28:25
Matt. 6:21
Luke 12:31-34
Rom. 13:14
Gal. 5:16
Eph. 2:3
Titus 2:12; 3:3
James 1:13-16; 4:2, 3
I John 2:16
Jude 18
I Pet. 1:14; 4:2, 3

Discipline
Prov. 3:11, 12; 13:24; 19:18;
  22:6, 15; 23:13; 29:15
I Cor. 5:1-13; 11:29-34
II Cor. 2:1-11
Eph. 6:1-4
I Tim. 4:7
Heb. 12:7-11

Divorce
Gen. 2:24
Deut. 24:1-4
Isa. 50:1
Jer. 3:1
Mal. 2:16
Matt. 5:31, 32; 19:3-8
Mark 10:3-5
I Cor. 7:10-24, 33-34, 39-40

Envy
Titus 3:3
James 3:14-16
I Pet. 2:1

Family
Gen. 2:18, 24
Ex. 20:12

Doubt
James 1:6-8

A. Husband/Wife
Gen. 2:18, 24
Eph. 5:22-33
Col. 3:18-21
I Pet. 3:1-17
I Tim. 2:11-15

Drunkenness
Prov. 20:1; 23:29-35; 31:4-6
23:20
Eph. 5:18
I Pet. 4:3

B. Parent/Child
Gen. 2:24
II Cor. 12:14
Eph. 6:1-4
I Tim. 3:4, 5

Forgiveness
Prov. 17:9
Matt. 6:14, 15; 18:15-17
Mark 11:25
Luke 17:3-10
Eph. 4:32
Col. 3:13
James 5:15
I John 1:8-10

Father (see Family)

Fear
Gen. 3:10
Prov. 10:24; 29:25
Matt. 10:26-31
II Tim. 1:7
Heb. 2:14, 15
I Pet. 3:6, 13, 14
I John 4:18

Friendship
Prov. 27:6, 10; 17:9, 17
John 15:13-15

Gifts
Rom. 12:3-8
I Cor. 12–14
I Pet. 4:10, 11

Gossip
Prov. 10:18; 11:13; 18:8;
20:19; 26:20-22
James 4:11

Homosexuality
Gen. 19
Lev. 18:22; 20:13
Rom. 1:26-32
I Cor. 6:9-11
I Tim 1:10

Grief
Prov. 14:13; 15:13
Eph. 4:30
I Thess. 4:13-18

Hope
Prov. 10:28; 13:12
Rom. 15:4, 5
I Thess. 1:3; 4:13-18
Heb. 6:11, 18, 19

Habit
Prov. 19:19
Isa. 1:10-17
Jer. 13:23; 22:21
Rom. 6–7
Gal. 5:16-21
I Tim., book of
Heb. 5:13ff.
I Pet. 2:14, 19

Humility
Prov. 3:34; 15:33; 16:19; 22:4;
29:23
Gal. 6:1, 2
Phil. 2:1-11
James 4:6, 10
I Pet. 5:6, 7

Jealousy (see Envy)

Laziness
Prov. 12:24, 27; 13:4;
15:19; 18:9; 26:13-16
Matt. 25:26

Listening
Prov. 5:1, 2, 13; 13:18; 15:31;
18:13

Lying
Ex. 20:16
Prov. 12:19, 22
Eph. 4:25
Col. 3:9

Love
Prov. 10:12; 17:19
Matt. 5:44; 22:39, 40
Rom. 13:10
I Cor. 13
I Pet. 1:22
I John 4:10, 19; 5:2, 3
II John 5, 6

Life-dominating Problems
I Cor. 6:9-12
Eph. 5:18
Rev. 21:8; 22:15

Lust (see Desire)

Mother (see Family)

Obedience
  I Sam. 15:22
  Luke 17:9, 10
  Acts 4:19; 5:29
  Eph. 6:1
  Heb. 5:8; 13:17
  I Pet. 1:22

Put-off/Put-on (see Change)

Reconciliation
  Matt. 5:23, 24; 18:15-17
  Luke 17:3-10

Peace
  Prov. 3:1, 2; 16:7
  John 14:27
  Rom. 5:1; 12:18; 14:19
  Phil. 4:6-9
  Col. 3:15
  Heb. 12:14

Repentance
  Luke 3:8-14; 24:47
  Acts 3:19; 5:31; 17:30; 26:20
  II Cor. 7:10; 12:21

Pride
  Prov. 8:13; 11:2; 13:10; 16:18;
    18:12; 21:24; 27:1; 29:23

Resentment
  Prov. 26:24-26
  Heb. 12:15

Reward/Punishment
Prov. 13:24; 22:15; 29:15;
II Cor. 2:6; 10:6
Heb. 10:35; 11:26
II John 8

Slander (see Gossip)

Stealing
Ex. 20:15
Prov. 20:10, 23; 29:24; 30:7-9
Eph. 4:28

Sexuality
Gen. 2:25
I Cor. 7:1-5

Work
Gen. 2:5-15; 3:17-19
Prov. 14:23; 18:9; 21:5; 22:29;
24:27; 31:10-31
I Cor. 15:58
Col. 3:22-24
I Thess. 4:11
II Thess. 13:6-15

Shame
Gen. 2:25
Prov. 11:2; 13:18
I Cor. 4:14
I Pet. 3:16

Worry
Prov. 12:25; 14:30; 17:22
Matt. 6:24-34
Phil. 4:6, 7
I Pet. 5:6, 7